T0194292

Knowing the Bible Through Powerful Poems, Prayers and Declarations.

GENESIS PART 1

Melecia Davis-Gibbs

WESTBOW
PRESS®
A DIVISION OF THOMAS NELSON
& ZONDERVAN

Scripture quotations are taken from the King James Version of the Bible

This book is a work of non-fiction. Unless otherwise noted, the author and the publisher make no explicit guarantees as to the accuracy of the information contained in this book and in some cases, names of people and places have been altered to protect their privacy.

WestBow Press books may be ordered through booksellers or by contacting:

WestBow Press
A Division of Thomas Nelson & Zondervan
1663 Liberty Drive
Bloomington, IN 47403
www.westbowpress.com
1 (866) 928-1240

Because of the dynamic nature of the Internet, any web addresses or links contained in this book may have changed since publication and may no longer be valid. The views expressed in this work are solely those of the author and do not necessarily reflect the views of the publisher, and the publisher hereby disclaims any responsibility for them.

This book is a work of non-fiction. Unless otherwise noted, the author and the publisher make no explicit guarantees as to the accuracy of the information contained in this book and in some cases, names of people and places have been altered to protect their privacy.

Any people depicted in stock imagery provided by Getty Images are models, and such images are being used for illustrative purposes only. Certain stock imagery © Getty Images.

ISBN: 978-1-9736-5096-6 (sc)
ISBN: 978-1-9736-5095-9 (e)

Print information available on the last page.

WestBow Press rev. date: 4/29/2019

ALL COMPOSED THROUGH THE DIRECTION OF THE HOLY SPIRIT

Melecia Davis-Gibbs

DEDICATION

This book is dedicated to my loving parents Lorington and Annmarie who introduced me to the Bible and taught me the value of discipline, dedication and integrity.

Contents

INTRODUCTION

"Man shall not live by bread alone but by every word that proceedeth out of the mouth of God." This was stated by Moses as recorded in the Old Testament of the Bible (Deuteronomy 8:3) and then repeated by Jesus Christ in the gospels found in the New Testament. (Matthew 4:4)

Questions for you, the reader.

- Do you find the Bible a bit difficult to read at times?
- Have you ever struggled just to get through reading a chapter of the Bible especially from the older versions?

Well this book is just for you!

What is the Bible?

The Bible is the most influential and powerful book ever written. It is the written Word of God and contains sixty six books that gives us an understanding of God's character and power. The Bible is divided into two Testaments namely the Old Testament, containing thirty nine books and the New Testament containing twenty seven books.

Reading and abiding by the precepts of this dynamic book, the Bible has brought enlightenment, salvation, healing and prosperity to the lives of its readers as they encounter God through its pages.

The Bible however, is not always easy to read; as a young Christian, my mentor Rupert Bailey once said to me to, "keep reading the Bible even when you don't understand it and the Holy Spirit will help you'. I have proven this to be true. The Holy Spirit is here to help us to understand its truths. It was the Holy Spirit who directed me to compose these poems, prayers and declarations, to help increase your knowledge of the Bible and to build your spiritual life.

The Content and Format of this book

This book consist of twenty-five powerful poems, prayers and declarations that focuses on the significant events in Genesis chapter one to twenty five and some lessons to learn from the chapters. The poems are based on the Bible, chapter to chapter of Genesis; it is a retelling of the stories in poetic form.

In each chapter of this book you will find a poem, followed by some lessons to learn, a focus Psalm that is fairly applicable to the text in Genesis by content or similar chapter, and a short prayer and declaration; each chapter ends with additional prayers and declarations and a short quiz

Benefits of this Book

- To help unfold the interesting stories of Genesis in a creative and poetic manner.
- To guide you in discovering profound information embedded in each chapter of Genesis.
- To stir your zeal and interest in reading the scriptures.

- To help uncover and understand the stories in the book of Genesis and recall them easily due to its poetic nature;
- To guide you in prayers and declarations based on scripture
- To increase your knowledge of some applicable Psalms
- To grasp lessons from the scripture applicable today

Reasons for writing this book

One of the reasons I wrote this book was to use the gift God has given me, to make a positive contribution to your spiritual walk with God and to stir your interest in searching the pages of your Bible, in order to know God more.

Invitation

It is my pleasure to invite you to get ready to turn the pages of this book slowly as you read, meditate and talk with God.

SECTION 1

POEM PRAYERS AND DECLARATIONS BASED ON CREATION AND THE LIFE OF NOAH

Genesis 1-11

In the beginning God created the heaven and the earth Genesis 1:1

GENESIS 1
POEM, PRAYERS AND DECLARATIONS

POEM
In The Beginning, God!

In the beginning, God,
Yes in the beginning God!

In the beginning, God created the heaven
In the beginning, God created the earth
In the beginning God
Yes, in the beginning, God.

Let there be light He said
Let there be light
God created the day
God created the night.

He separates water from land
That He called earth and sea.
Filled them with all kinds of living things
Look around and see.

Fishes in the water
Trees on land
On the sixth day
He created man.

In the beginning, God, yes
In the beginning God
Creator of the heaven
Creator of the earth
In the beginning, God, yes
In the beginning God!

LESSON

- ➤ God is Creator.
- ➤ God is creative - look at nature's variety and beauty.
- ➤ God is supernatural, He is all powerful.

PRAYER

I praise the Creator of the heaven
I praise the Creator of the earth
I praise the Maker of the land and sea
Who knew me before my birth.

You worked six days and rested on the seventh
I will do likewise as my God in heaven.

DECLARATION

There is no other creator of the heavens and the earth.
Jehovah, Creator of the heaven and earth is my God

FOCUS PSALM
PSALM 1:1-3 AND PSALM 8:3-9

*1 Blessed is the man that walketh not in the counsel
of the ungodly nor standeth in the way of sinners,
nor sitteth in the seat of the scornful.
2 But his delight is in the law of the Lord and in
his law doth he meditates day and night.
3 And he shall be like a tree planted by the rivers of
water, that bringeth forth fruit in his season, his leaf shall
not wither, and whatsoever he doeth shall prosper*

PSALM 8:3-9

3 When I consider thy heavens, the work of thy fingers, the moon and the stars, which thou hast ordained; 4 What is man, that thou art mindful of him? and the son of man, that thou visitest him? 5 For thou hast made him a little lower than the angels, and hast crowned him with glory and honour. 6 Thou madest him to have dominion over the works of thy hands; thou hast put all things under his feet: 7 All sheep and oxen, yea, and the beasts of the field; 8 The fowl of the air, and the fish of the sea, and whatsoever passeth through the paths of the seas. 9 O Lord our Lord, how excellent is thy name in all the earth!

ADDITIONAL PRAYERS AND DECLARATIONS BASED ON GENESIS 1

1. Praises to God the Creator of heaven and earth [1:1].
2. Heavenly Father, remove any kind of darkness (of depression, frustration, etc) that may overshadow my life in the name of Jesus Christ [1:2].
3. Lord, let the Holy Spirit move upon my life as He moved upon the earth and do great things, and fix anything in my life that needs fixing in the name of Jesus Christ.
4. Lord, shine your light in my life and dispel all darkness in the name of Jesus Christ [1:3].
5. Lord, let good things happen in my life today and do a mighty work [1:4].
6. Lord, let me be spiritually fruitful and productive in the name of Jesus Christ [1:11].
7. Heavenly Father, take charge of and rule as king of my life as the sun rules the day in the name of Jesus Christ [1:16].

8. Lord, take away any fear I may have of any animal/insect in the name of Jesus as you have given me dominion over these things [1:28].
9. Lord, Creator of the world, create new things in my life and let your goodness be evident in the name of Jesus.
10. Lord, bless me and my family as we produce fruit for your kingdom in the name of Jesus [1:22].
11. I declare, I am filled with the light of God's Word.
12. I am fearfully and wonderfully made in the image of God [1:27]
13. I declare good things are happening in my life.
14. I have authority and dominion over the animals of this earth; therefore I shall not be afraid of any insect in the name of Jesus Christ [1:28].
15. I will not fear any animal because I have dominion over them in the name of Jesus Christ [1:26].

GENESIS 1 QUIZ
ANSWER TRUE OR FALSE

1. In the beginning God created the heavens only.   True/False
2. The earth was without form and void and
   darkness was upon the face of the earth.   True/False
3. God said let there be darkness and there
   was light.   True/False
4. God called the firmament heaven.   True/False
5. On the fifth day God created fowls.   True/False
6. God created the stars on the sixth day.   True/False
7. Cattles were created on the fifth day.   True/False
8. Man was made in the image of God
   on the fourth day.   True/False
9. God united the light and darkness.   True/False
10. God called the dry land earth and the
    gathering of water streams.   True/False
11. God made two great lights, the greater
    rule by day and the lesser rule by night.   True/False
12. God called everything He created good.   True/False

GENESIS 2-3
POEM, PRAYERS AND DECLARATIONS

POEM
The First Temptation

The Garden of Eden a Beautiful Place

The Garden of Eden, a beautiful place
There God put Adam and Eve, the beginning of the human race.
A place where three rivers run through
The river of Pison, Gisho, and Hiddekel too.

The Garden of Eden, a beautiful place
Of any fruit of the garden, the man could eat
All, except the fruit of the tree of knowledge of good and evil
That fruit was forbidden to touch his teeth.

But here comes the serpent, the one we call the devil
with sin on his mind and evil in his heart.
Eve, he said, 'just eat the forbidden fruit, you will not die'.
But we all know that was definitely a lie.

Eve gazed at the fruit with a desire to be wise
With such a temptation, Adam and Eve
ate the fruit to their demise.

It was in the Garden of Eden, that beautiful place
Man was tempted and swiftly fell from grace.

LESSONS

> ➢ It does not matter where we are, how beautiful a place is, we are not exempt from temptation.
> ➢ We sin when we yield to temptation.
> ➢ The devil is a liar and seeks to lead us to sin against God.

GOD IN GENESIS

> ❖ God is caring - He saw that Adam needed help and companionship so He provided it.
> ❖ God is instructive - He delegated responsibilities to Adam, to name the animals.
> ❖ God is a disciplined and principled God- He gave Adam instructions with an expectation of his obedience.
> ❖ God will chastise His people when necessary.

PRAYER

Lord in my season of plenty, keep me temptation free
Keep me from the devil and his evil schemes.

DECLARATION

I refuse to give into temptation.
I refuse to tempt my fellow men to sin.
I choose to believe the Word of God.

FOCUS PSALM
PSALM 2:10-11

Be wise now, therefore, o ye kings, be
instructed, ye judges of the earth
Serve the Lord with fear and rejoice with trembling

ADDITIONAL PRAYERS AND DECLARATIONS BASED ON GENESIS 2

1. Blessed be God Almighty who made heaven and earth [2:1].
2. Breath of God, breathe on me and revive me today, to good health [2:7].
3. Lord, supply my needs as you did for Adam in the name of Jesus Christ [2:9].
4. There shall be enough food in my house because God is my provider [2:9].
5. Lord, help me to follow your commandments whole heartedly in Jesus name.
6. Lord, bless me with a godly companion, since it is not good for me be alone in the name of Jesus Christ [2:18].
7. Lord, help the husbands/wives to properly adapt the principle of leaving parents and cleaving to their spouse in a godly manner in the name of Jesus Christ [2:24].
8. Lord, let each couple operate in unity as they become one flesh in the name of Jesus Christ [2:24].
9. Lord, guide the newlyweds among us in their marital relationships and relationships with in-laws in the name of Jesus Christ [2:24].
10. Lord, provide for me a good helpmate, a good life partner in Jesus name.
11. I shall take time to rest on a weekly basis [2:2].
12. God is my Creator [2:7].

13. I will be a good life partner in Jesus name.
14. My marriage is characterized by unity, love, passion, respect and trust.

ADDITIONAL PRAYERS AND DECLARATIONS BASED ON GENESIS 3

1. Lord, help me to be vigilant to recognize and resist the subtle schemes of the devil in the name of Jesus Christ [3:1].
2. Heavenly Father, help me to shun the advice and instruction of the evil one [3:2].
3. I reject every lie the devil whispered to me in the name of Jesus Christ [3:4]
4. Lord, open my eyes to see and recognize the evil one when he comes; and strengthen me to resist him in the name of Jesus Christ [3:4-5].
5. Lord, in the name of Jesus Christ forgive me of every sinful deed I have done [3:6].
6. Lord, in the name of Jesus Christ open my ears to hear your voice when you call [3:8].
7. Lord teach me to know and recognize your voice and to listen to you when you speak [3:10]
8. I shall hear the voice of the Lord and be guided by Him [3:10].
9. 9. I will own up to my wrongs and not blame others for it. Lord, forgive me for all the wrongs I have done against you in Jesus name. [3:10].
10. I will accept responsibility for my actions [3:10].
11. By the grace of God I will not be deceived by the enemy, in Jesus name [3:13].
12. O Lord, thank you for giving me victory over the enemy in Jesus name [3:15].
13. I will walk in victory, not defeat, in Jesus name.
14. With the knowledge of good and evil, I choose to do good in Jesus name [3:22].

ADDITIONAL READING
HEBREW 4:4

ADAM IN OTHER BOOKS OF BIBLE
Luke 3:38
Romans 5:13
I Corinthians 15:22, 45
1 Timothy 2:14
Jude 14

GENESIS 2 QUIZ
ANSWER TRUE OR FALSE

1. God rested on the seventh day and sanctified it.   True/False
2. Man was created on the seventh day.   True/False
3. The Lord formed man from the dust of the earth and breathe into his nostril.   True/False
4. The Lord planted a garden eastward of Eden.   True/False
5. The tree of life and the tree of the knowledge of good and evil were in the Garden of Eden.   True/False
6. A river went out of the garden and was parted in four.   True/False
7. Hiddekel is the name of the plant in the garden.   True/False
8. Adam was commanded not to eat of the tree of good and evil.   True/False
9. It is not good for a man to be alone.   True/False
10. Pison passed through the land of Havilah where there was gold.   True/False

GENESIS 3 QUIZ
ANSWER TRUE OR FALSE

1. The serpent was less subtle than any beast
   in the field.   True/False
2. The woman took the apple and gave her
   husband to eat.   True/False
3. Adam heard God's voice in the garden and
   was afraid.   True/False
4. God cursed the serpent to eat dust all the
   days of his life.   True/False
5. Adam called his wife Eve because she
   was not a mother.   True/False
6. God drove Adam and Eve out of the garden.   True/False
7. The ground was cursed because Adam
   disobeyed God.   True/False
8. In sorrow the woman would have children.   True/False
9. God placed a cherubim east of the Garden of Eden
   and a flaming sword to keep the tree of life safe.   True/False
10. The Lord made coats of skin and clothed
    Adam and Eve.   True/False

GENESIS 4-5
POEM, PRAYERS AND DECLARATIONS

POEM
Sin Lies At Your Door

Be careful, sin lies at your door
Sin lies at your door.
Adam and Eve joyful parents of two sons, Cain and Abel
Sooner or later, their joy would be snuffed out, this is not a fable.

Be careful, sin lies at your door
Sin lies at your door
Cain and Abel grew to become skillful men in their profession
Cain a farmer and Abel a shepherd man.

Be careful, sin lies at your door
Sin lies at your door
Abel brought his offering to the Lord that God accepted.
Cain brought his offering to the Lord, but woe, God rejected!

Be careful, sin lies at your door
Sin lies at your door.
Cain now filled with red-hot anger, perhaps silent rage
"Abel, just you wait, I will definitely get
you! I will slay you one day".

Be careful, sin lies at your door
Sin lies at your door
Cain filled with wrath, rage and evil sinful thoughts
Because God rejected the offering he brought.

Be careful, sin lies at your door
Sin lies at your door.
Cain slay Abel; Abel is dead
"I'm not my brother's keeper"! That Cain said

Be careful, sin lies at your door
Sin lies at your door.
Farmer became a murderer, in just one day
The blood of Abel cries out, that Cain slay.

Be careful, sin lies at your door,
Sin lies at your door.
Let go of the wrath, let go of the rage
Give it to God, that's the better way.

LESSON

- ➢ We should give God our best offering.
- ➢ Uncontrolled anger can lead to sin.
- ➢ We must look out for the best interest of our love ones, and be our brother's keeper.
- ➢ Sin comes with terrible consequences.

GOD IN GENESIS

- ➢ God is God- He expects to be worshipped and offering be given Him.
- ➢ God is corrective – He corrected Cain; He communicates with us even when we do wrong.
- ➢ God is just - God punished Cain for murdering his brother. Cain was not even remorseful.
- ➢ God knows what is in our heart- He knew what was in Cain's heart.

PRAYER

Lord, thank you for showing me my faults.
I submit to you now.
Help me not to follow the way of Cain, Adams son

DECLARATION

I refused to be controlled by anger, wrath, and rage.
Instead, I will do what is right and trust in the Lord.

FOCUS PSALM
PSALM 4:4-4

Stand in awe and sin not, commune with your
own heart upon your bed and be still
Offer the sacrifices of righteousness
and put your trust in the Lord

ADDITIONAL PRAYERS AND DECLARATIONS BASED ON GENESIS 4

1. Praise the Lord who watches over his people.
2. Lord, I offer to you sacrifices of praise today [4:3].
3. Lord, let my offering of worship, prayer and fasting be acceptable to you in the name of Jesus [4:4].
4. Lord, help me to deal with correction in a godly manner in the name of Jesus [4:5].
5. I shall do well in ministry and service to God in the name of Jesus [4:7].
6. I reject every evil thought to do anyone harm, in the name of Jesus [4:8].
7. Lord, help me to do good and not to harm my family in the name of Jesus Christ [4:8].
8. I shall not follow the bad attitude and behavior of Cain in the name of Jesus [4:8]
9. Unlike Cain, I shall be my brother's keeper [4:9].
10. Lord, help me to offer a pleasing sacrifice to you, in the name of Jesus Christ.

ADDITIONAL PRAYERS AND DECLARATIONS BASED ON GENESIS 5

1. Praise God, I am created in His likeness [5:1].
2. Bless me O Lord as you blessed my fore- parents [5:2].

3. Lord, bless me with health and strength to fulfill my days here on earth in the name of Jesus.
4. Lord, help me to walk with you in righteousness and truth, in the name of Jesus [5:22].
5. I shall walk with God in a righteous manner, as Enoch walked, in the name of Jesus [5:22].
6. Lord, provide persons who will encourage us concerning our work and labour for the You, in the name of Jesus Christ [5:29].
7. Lord, teach us how to comfort and support each other in our family in the name of Jesus Christ [5:29].
8. Lord, forgive us and break every curse from off our lives in the name of Jesus Christ [5:29].
9. I declare the curse is broken in the name of Jesus Christ [5:29].
10. I will bring comfort to those around me that are in need, in Jesus name [5:29].

RELEVANT SCRIPTURE READING ON GENESIS 4

Hebrews 11:4

Matthew 23:25

I John 3:12-15

Jude 11

Hebrew 12:24

RELEVANT SCRIPTURE READING GENESIS 5

Jude 14-16

Hebrews 11:5

Hebrews 9:27

ABEL AND CAIN IN OTHER BOOKS OF THE BIBLE

1 John 3:12
Jude 11
Matthew 23:35
Luke 11:51
Hebrew 12:24

GENESIS 4 QUIZ
ANSWER TRUE OR FALSE

1. Abel was a shepherd and Cain was a farmer.   True/False
2. Able was younger than Cain.   True/False
3. The Lord respected Abel's offering but not Cain.   True/False
4. The Lord told Cain that if he had done well
    He would have accepted him.   True/False
5. Cain got very angry and cursed his mother.   True/False
6. Cain said he is his brother's keeper.   True/False
7. Cain killed his brother Abel.   True/False
8. God said Cain would be a fugitive and vagabond. True/False
9. Cain built a city and called it after the name
    of his son Enoch.   True/False
10. Eve said God gave her Seth in place of Cain.   True/False

GENESIS 5 QUIZ
ANSWER TRUE OR FALSE

1. Man was created in the likeness of God.   True/False
2. Adam was 130 yrs old when Seth was born.   True/False
3. Caiman who lived 910 years was Seth grandson.   True/False
4. At the age of 82 yrs old Lamech had a
    son called Noah.   True/False
5. Methuselah was Noah's grandfather
    and Lamech's father.   True/False

GENESIS 6-7
POEM, PRAYERS AND DECLARATIONS

POEM
Noah Found Grace In The Eyes Of The Lord

Evil was rampant, wickedness great
But in God's eyes, Noah found grace.
Violence increase, corruption high
But Noah stood righteous, in God's sight.

God said, "Noah I want you to build an ark
Warn the people rain is going to fall.
No ordinary rain, but a flood on the land
Washing this earth, with my mighty hand".

Noah builds the ark, animal and family went in
But all other men, chose the way of sin.
Yes Noah, found grace in the eyes of the Lord
He warned the people, but they rejected his word.

God shuts the ark, the rain came down
Animals died, humanity wiped out.
All flesh died, fowl and cattle
Beasts and every creeping thing, without a battle.

All died except those in the ark
Because Noah found grace, in the eyes of the Lord.

LESSON

It's possible to live a clean life in a dirty world.

GOD IN GENESIS

- ❖ God is holy – He hates sin.
- ❖ God is objective – He is able to look at a situation and make a fair decision. Amidst the sinfulness He found grace with Noah. [6:8]
- ❖ God is detailed – He gave detailed instruction on how to build the ark.
- ❖ God is caring – even for the animals in the midst of judgment. [6:19-20]
- ❖ God is a covenant maker- He made a covenant with Noah [6:18]

PRAYER

May I find grace in thy sight O Lord, in these evil days.
May my life be pleasing unto thee, in every
single way in the name of Jesus Christ.

DECLARATION

I choose to be pure and holy.
I chose to be right and true.
I choose to walk in my integrity.

FOCUS PSALM
PSALM 7:8-9

The Lord shall judge the people; judge me O Lord according to
my righteousness and according to mine integrity that is in me
Oh, let the wickedness of the wicked come to
an end, but establish the just, for the righteous
God trieth the hearts and reins.

ADDITIONAL PRAYER POINTS AND DECLARATIONS BASED ON GENESIS 6

1. Lord, touch my life and may I find grace in your sight in the name of Jesus Christ [6:8].
2. Lord, help me to walk with you as Noah walked with you in the name of Jesus Christ [6:9].
3. May we be righteous and holy in our generation as Noah was in his in the name of Jesus [6:9].
4. Lord in this world of wickedness and violence direct us as you directed Noah in the name of Jesus Christ [6:13].
5. Lord, flood our land with your power and break the yoke of wickedness in Jesus' name [6:11].
6. God, your Spirit will not always strive with man; save the unsaved in my family in the name of Jesus [6:3].
7. Lord, put an end to the wickedness in our family and nation in the name of Jesus [6:5].
8. Lord, forgive us, I repent on behalf of our family, friends and nation; forgive us for causing you grief in the name of Jesus [6:6]
9. The land is corrupt and filled with violence but have mercy O Lord in the name of Jesus [6:11].
10. Let the judgment of God be upon the wicked who reject God and will not change [6:13]

ADDITIONAL PRAYER POINTS AND DECLARATIONS BASED ON GENESIS 7

1. Lord, may I obey you as Noah obeyed, in the name of Jesus Christ [7:5].
2. Lord, may I do what you direct me to do, in the name of Jesus Christ [7:5].
3. Lord, flood my life with your power and flush out every evil thought, attitude and deeds in the name of Jesus Christ [7:6].
4. Lord, cleanse me, my family and church from all uncleanness in the name of Jesus Christ [.
5. Lord, may our home be like the ark Noah built, a place of safety and security in Jesus name [7:7].
6. Lord, keep us safe and secure from natural disasters such as earthquakes, tsunami, hurricane and floods in Jesus name [7:7].
7. Lord, save every member of my household as you saved Noah and his family in Jesus name [7:16].
8. We are safe and secure in Jesus name [7:23].
9. I declare that every member of my family shall be saved in Jesus name [7:23].
10. My life is filled with the power of God.

NOAH IN SOME OTHER BOOKS OF THE BIBLE

2 Peter 2:5
Hebrew 11:7
1 Peter 3:20
Matthew 24:37-39
Luke 17:26-27

GENESIS 6 QUIZ.
ANSWER TRUE OR FALSE

1. God said 'My Spirit will always strive with man.'   True/False
2. There were giants in the days of Noah.   True/False
3. The earth was filled with corruption.   True/False
4. God said the earth was filled with violence and
    He will destroy all flesh.   True/False
5. God said He would establish a covenant
    with Noah's wife.   True/False
6. God saw that the imagination of the thoughts
    of man was only evil.   True/False
7. Noah found grace in the eyes of the Lord.   True/False
8. Noah had four sons, Shem, Seth,
    Ham and Japhcth.   True/False
9. God told Noah to make an ark of gopher wood.   True/False
10. God told Noah to build the ark of lower,
    second and third stories.   True/False

GENESIS 7 QUIZ
ANSWER TRUE OR FALSE

1. Noah did not do all that the Lord commanded.   True/False
2. Both clean and unclean beast went into the ark.   True/False
3. For forty days and forty nights, rain fell
    upon the earth.   True/False
4. All flying animals were destroyed in the flood.   True/False
5. It was God and not Noah who shut the
    door of the ark.   True/False
6. Only eight persons went into the ark before
    the flood.   True/False
7. Both male and female animals went in the ark.   True/False

8. All high hills were covered with water
    because of the flood.   True/False
9. All the animals died in the ark.   True/False
10. Noah was sixty years old when the flood came.   True/False

RELEVANT SCRIPTURE READING ON GENESIS 6

Matthew 5:19
Romans 1:28
2 Peter 2:5
Romans 5:12
Hebrews 1:7

RELEVANT SCRIPTURE READING ON GENESIS 7

2 Peter 2:9
Luke 17:27
Matthew 24:39
2 Peter 2:5
1 Peter 3:20

GENESIS 8-9
POEM, PRAYERS AND DECLARATIONS

POEM
Rainbow

Rainbow, rainbow, beautiful rainbow
A sign of the covenant of man with God;
God blessed Noah and his sons
Be fruitful and multiply on this land.

Green herbs are there for you to eat
Everything that lived shall be your meat.
The blood of the animals, do not eat
It is forbidden to drink the blood of beast.

No more floods to cut off all flesh from the land
Rainbow, a sign of the covenant, between God and man;
A bow in the cloud will remind me of this covenant
No more, destroy the earth by waters, abundant.

LESSON

> ➤ After any disaster we can still look
> to God for encouragement.

GOD IN GENESIS

❖ God will provide for His people.
❖ God wants us to be fruitful and productive.
❖ God is tender hearted [8:21].
❖ God remembers his people in times of judgment –
He remembered Noah and his family [8:1, 15]
❖ God is a covenant maker [9:11-17]

PRAYER

God of Noah hear my cry
Help me to be fruitful and multiply.
Lord, flood my life with your word and
power, in the name of Jesus Christ.

DECLARATION

I am productive and shall bear fruits in the name of Jesus Christ.

FOCUS PSALM
PSALM 8:3-4

*When I consider thy heavens and the work of thy fingers,
the moon and the stars which thou hast ordained
What is man that thou art mindful of him? And
the son of man that thou visits him?*

ADDITIONAL PRAYER POINTS AND DECLARATIONS BASED ON GENESIS 8 AND 9

1. Lord, remember me as you remembered Noah in Jesus name [8:1].
2. Lord, wherever there is a flood in this world, let the waters recede and remember your people in Jesus name [8:4].
3. Lord, as Noah opened the window of the ark, open windows of opportunity for me in Jesus name [8:4].
4. When the dove Noah sent found no place to rest, Noah pulled him in, even so Lord pull me in, closer to you in times of weakness in the name of Jesus Christ [8:9].
5. Lord, I honour you for the promise you made, that you will not curse the ground anymore because of the wickedness of man [8:21].
6. God, bless me and my family as you blessed Noah, may we be fruitful in spiritual and material things in Jesus name [9:1].
7. Let the fear of man be upon every animal of the earth [9:2].
8. Lord, I worship you for I am made in the image of God [9:6].
9. Lord, God of Covenant, be praised for the rainbow that serves as a reminder that you will not destroy the earth by water [9:15-17].
10. Lord, as Noah planted a vineyard, may we plant your words in the hearts of men in Jesus name [9:20].
11. Lord, deliver us from drunkenness of wine and make us drunk in the Spirit in Jesus name [9:22].
12. Lord, in Jesus name help us to protect our parents and shield them in times of weakness as Shem and Japheth did [9:22-23].

GENESIS 8 QUIZ
ANSWER TRUE OR FALSE

1. After the flood the ark was upon the mountains of Ararat.   True/False

2. Noah sent a male dove to see if the waters were dried up.   True/False

3. At the end of forty days Noah opened the window of the ark.   True/False

4. Noah sent out a raven and a dove to see if the waters were abated.   True/False

5. After the flood every living thing outside the ark was destroyed except the whales.   True/False

6. The Lord said He would not curse the ground anymore for man's sake.   True/False

7. Noah built an altar and offered a burnt offering to God after he came out of the ark.   True/False

8. God was not pleased with the offering Noah gave him.   True/False

9. Noah's wife did not survive during the flood.   True/False

10. Noah's daughters- inlaws refused to enter the ark and therefore they were not saved.   True/False

GENESIS 9 QUIZ
ANSWER TRUE OR FALSE

1. God told Noah and his sons to be fruitful and multiply and replenish the earth.   True/False

2. God said the animals of the earth would fear Noah.   True/False

3. God gave a warning about the consequence of murder.   True/False

4. God told Noah he could eat meat but
   not the blood.   True/False
5. God made a covenant with Noah, his family
   and the living creatures on the earth that He
   will not destroy the earth by a flood.   True/False
6. The bow was a sign of the covenant God
   make with Shem.   True/False
7. Seth and Japheth took a garment and covered
   Noah nakedness.   True/False
8. God said He would bring a cloud over the earth
   so that the bow can be seen.   True/False
9. Noah cursed Ham and blessed Canaan.   True/False
10. Noah lived 350 years after the flood.   True/False

RELEVANT SCRIPTURE READING ON GENESIS 9

James 3:7

Acts 1:27

Ephesians 5:18

READ GENESIS 10

*Now these are the generations of the sons of Noah, Shem, Ham,
and Japheth; and unto them were sons born after the flood…..*

GENESIS 11
POEM, PRAYERS AND DECLARATIONS

POEM
Babel

The whole earth, was of one language, one speech
In Shinar to build a city and high tower, in heaven's reach
God came down to see the city and tower
By this sight, God decided to scatter them by his power.

Confused in language, they scattered abroad
Not to remain in one city but to inhabit the world
The name of the city was called Babel
Because, there the Lord confounded the language of the people.

LESSON

➤ It is possible for a group of persons to accomplish difficult tasks when they are unified.

➤ Disobedience to God leads to the judgment of God.

➤ It is difficult to communicate when we are not speaking the same language.

➤ Confusion of language can create major problems in a family and organization.

GOD IN GENESIS

❖ God confused their language because He wanted His people to inhabit the earth.

❖ God is sovereign – He has a plan for His people and will do what it takes for it to be accomplished.

PRAYER

Confuse the language of my enemies O Lord
Scatter them, scatter them scatter them abroad
In the name of Jesus Christ.

DECLARATION

I refuse to go against the will of God.

FOCUS PSALM
PSALM 11:4

The Lord is in his holy temple, the Lord's throne is in heaven;
his eyes behold, his eyelids try, the children of men.

ADDITIONAL PRAYER POINTS AND DECLARATIONS BASED ON GENESIS 11

1. Lord, in Jesus name, may my family be of one speech and language as we communicate with each other [11;1].
2. May we as a family work together in unity in the name of Jesus Christ [11:3].
3. Lord, come down and see what is happening in our family and nation and remove any obstacle to your will in Jesus name [11:5-7].
4. Lord, separate us from anything that is a hindrance to our development in Jesus name [11:8].
5. I declare, I shall walk in the will of God in the name of Jesus Christ.
6. Lord, help us to build houses and businesses for the benefit of our families well being and prosperity in Jesus name. [11:3].
7. Lord, bless our family members with visas to be able to travel and spread Your Word across the world in the name of Jesus Christ [11:4].
8. Lord, may we be united for the right reasons and be as one so that we can do greater things for the kingdom in Jesus name [11:6].
9. Lord, any decision that we have made that is not your will, let it be clearly known in the name of Jesus [11:9].
10. Lord, redirect us to your will for our lives in any area where we have strayed in Jesus name
11. Lord, come and fix our lives, guide us and redirect us where necessary in Jesus name [11:9].
12. I declare, I will walk in the will of God for my life.
13. We will do what the Lord has directed us to do in Jesus name.
14. We will not walk contrary to God's purpose for our lives in Jesus name.

GENESIS 10-11
ANSWER TRUE OR FALSE

1. Nimrod, Cush son was a mighty hunter.   True/False
2. The whole earth was of one language and
    one speech.   True/False
3. The people planned to use brick for stone and
    slime for mortar to build the city.   True/False
4. The Lord confused the people's language and
    scattered them.   True/False
5. The people decided to build a city and a tower
    that would reach into the heavens.   True/False
6. The Lord scattered the people because they
    were corrupt and evil.   True/False
7. Babel is the name of the city where God
    confused the language of the people.   True/False
8. Abram's brothers were Nahor and Lot.   True/False
9. Abram's father's name was Terah.   True/False
10. Terah took Abram and family and they
    left Ur to go to Canaan.   True/False

RELEVANT SCRIPTURE READING ON GENESIS

Luke 1:51
Hebrews 11:8
Hebrews 9:7

SECTION 2

POEM PRAYERS AND DECLARATIONS BASED ON THE LIFE OF ABRAHAM

GENESIS 12-25

Now the Lord had said to Abram get thee out of thy country and from thy kindred, and from thy father's house and unto a land I will show you. Gen 12:1

GENESIS 12
POEM, PRAYERS AND DECLARATIONS

POEM
Get Out

Get out of thy country, get out!
Get out of thy father's house.
Get out! I will bless thee and make thee great
Get out get out Abram, get out!

Abram took wife Sarai, Lot and family, left his homeland
They journeyed from Haran to Canaan
While in Canaan, the Lord appeared
Saying Abram, "I will bless thee and thy seed"
Therefore, Abram built an altar there.

Get out of this place, get out!
Get out of this place, thy father's house. Get
out! I will bless thee and make thee great
Get out get out Abram, get out!

Abram moved unto Bethel
Built an altar, pitched a tent,
He continued to journey towards the south
With famine in the land, to Egypt he sojourned.

The Egyptian noticed Sarah, Abrams' beautiful wife
Abram said "tell them you're just my
sister", of course, that's a lie
So beautiful to behold was his wife Sarah

Egyptian princes recommended this
beauty to their leader, Pharaoh.

Due to Sarai's beauty, Pharaoh treated Abram well
Gave him sheep oxen, asses, servant, and camels as well
But God was angry, He plagued Pharaoh's house
God was angry, He plagued Pharaohs' house.

"Abram! What have you done", Pharaoh sternly asked.
"Sarai is your wife, not your sister, alas!
Take your wife, go away
That God may release me from these plagues".

LESSON

> Know the voice of God and move as He directs you.
>> External and internal beauty can bring favour in our lives, but internal beauty is God's delight.
>> It is best to remove from our lives whatever we have that is not of God or in His will for us.

GOD IN GENESIS

❖ God warns people before He judges them.

❖ Be assured that God defends His people.

❖ God is a promise giver – He made promises to Abraham

❖ God is a defender and protector – He plagued Pharaoh's house because of Sarah.

PRAYER

Lord, take me out of any situation and
place that I should not be in.
Lord, bless us and make us great.
Guard and protect us in Jesus' name.

DECLARATION

I will move according to God's direction.

FOCUS PSALM
PSALM 12:1-2

*Help O Lord for the godly man ceaseth, for the
faithful, fail among the children of men.
They speak vanity everyone with is neighbor, with
flattering lips and a double heart do they speak.*

ADDITIONAL PRAYER POINTS AND DECLARATION BASED ON GENESIS 12

1. Lord, any place I am in my life that I should not be, let it be known and direct me where to go in Jesus name [12:1].
2. I will get out of any situation I should not be in, in Jesus name [12:1].
3. I will move when God says move no matter how difficult it may seem in the name of Jesus Christ [12:1].
4. Lord, as you promised Abram, make me great, bless me and make me a blessing in Jesus name [12:3].
5. Lord, as Abram found the courage to move when you said move, so give us courage to do the same in the name of Jesus [12:5].
6. Lord, reveal yourself and confirm your promises to me and my family as you did for Abraham in the name of Jesus [12:7].
7. The promises God made to me will come to pass in the name of Jesus [12:7].
8. Lord, in times of famine, show me where to go and what to do to provide for my family in Jesus name [12:10].
9. I refuse to put my family in danger [12:12]
10. I will continue to call on the name of the Lord [12:8].
11. Lord, hear my cry, lead and direct my path as I journey today, in Jesus name [12:9}
12. I will do what is necessary to protect my family, in Jesus name.
13. Lord, beautify me as you did Sarai with beauty, youthfulness and strength in Jesus name [12:15].

14. Lord, plague any Pharaoh in our lives and break their hold in Jesus name [12:15-17].

GENESIS 12 QUIZ
ANSWER TRUE OR FALSE

1. God commanded Abram to leave his father's house and go to a place He would show him.   True/False
2. Abram obeyed God and left the place called Haran with Lot at the age of seventy five years old.   True/False
3. God said He would bless Abram and make him great.   True/False
4. Lot went with Abram out of Sinai.   True/False
5. Abram built an altar after the Lord appeared to him.   True/False
6. Abram went to Egypt because there was war in Canaan.   True/False
7. The Lord plagued Pharaoh's house because of Sarai.   True/False
8. The Egyptians saw that Sarai was beautiful.   True/False
9. The prince introduced Sarai to Pharaoh and he took her in his house.   True/False
10. Pharaoh commanded that Abram and Sarai remain with him in Egypt.   True/False

RELEVANT SCRIPTURE READING ON GENESIS

Acts 7:2-3
Acts 3:25
Hebrews 11:8
Ephesians 4:25

GENESIS 13
POEM, PRAYERS AND DECLARATIONS

POEM
Riches And Strife

Riches, riches, riches
Strife, strife, strife
Riches, riches, riches
Strife, strife, strife.

Abram very rich
In cattle, silver, and gold
Riches, riches, riches
More, more, more.

Lot had plenty
Flocks, herds, tents
The land could not bear
These two rich men.

Herdsmen against herdsmen
That was the strife
Riches, riches, riches
Strife, strife, strife

Abram said, "Lot, the whole land is before us
Let's reject this strife
You go your way
I will go mine".

Lot chose Sodom and Gomorrah
In Canaan, Abram stayed
God blessed Abram,
More wealth, he gained.

Riches, riches, riches
Yes, no, no strife
Riches, riches, riches
Yes, no, no strife.

LESSONS

➢ People can cause strife in our family if we allow them.
➢ There is always a solution to strife.
➢ Riches can be a problem if it's not handled properly.
➢ When there is strife, try to resolve it as soon as possible.

GOD IN GENESIS

❖ God is observant - it was evident that He was watching how Abram dealt with the problem in his family. Ps 121:1
❖ God is a promise keeper and promise reminder - He promised Abram lands and again reminded him of this. Numbers 23:19
❖ God is a rewarder - He rewarded Abram for how he dealt with the situation. Hebrews 11:6

PRAYER

Lord, remove any strife from my family
Keep us as one, help us to walk in unity
in Jesus name. Amen.

DECLARATION

Strife shall not rule in my life.
I will try to live peaceably with all.
I will resolve any strife in my life.

FOCUS PSALM
PSALM 13:3-6

Consider and hear me O Lord my God, lighten
mine eyes, lest sleep the sleep of death
Lest mine enemies and those that trouble
me rejoice when I am moved
But I have trusted in thy mercy, my heart
shall rejoice in thy salvation
I will sing unto the Lord for He has dealt bountifully with me

ADDITIONAL PRAYER POINTS AND DECLARATIONS BASED ON GENESIS 13

1. Lord bless us as you blessed Abraham; with silver, gold and cattle (food) in Jesus name [13:1].
2. Lord, make me rich in spiritual and material possessions in the name of Jesus Christ. [13:1]
3. I reject poverty and receive wealth in Jesus name.
4. Heavenly Father, I call on the name of the Lord who is worthy to be praised.
5. Lord, resolve any strife among my family in Jesus name [13:6].
6. I reject any kind of strife in my life and family in the name of Jesus Christ [13:7]
7. My family and I will walk and live in peace in Jesus name. [13:7].
8. Lord, help me to make the right decision when face with difficult choices to make peace in Jesus name [13:10].
9. Lord, open my eyes to recognize that not all things that appear to be good are good for me. Help me to seek You earnestly before making major decisions in Jesus name [13:10]
10. Bless me and my family with good land and healthy children in Jesus name [13:15].

11. Lord, touch the hearts of the wicked among us and reveal yourself to them once again in Jesus name [13:13].
12. I put every sinner in my family/community before You, have mercy Lord God and save them in Jesus name [13:13].
13. I am blessed and my family is blessed, in Jesus name.
14. Like Abram, I will call upon the name of the Lord.

RELEVANT SCRIPTURE READING ON GENESIS

Philippians 2:14-15
Hebrews 12:14
2 Peter 2:7
Romans 4:16

GENESIS 13 QUIZ
ANSWER TRUE OR FALSE

1. Abram was very rich with cattle, silver and gold.   True/False
2. Abram built an altar in Bethel.   True/False
3. There was strife between Abram and Noah's herdsmen.   True/False
4. Abram said 'let there be no strife between us'.   True/False
5. Lot relocated to Sodom and Gomorrah.   True/False
6. Abram built an altar in Hebron.   True/False
7. The men of Sodom were wicked sinners before the Lord.   True/False
8. After Abram and Lot parted, Abram dwelt in Zoar.   True/False
9. The Lord appeared to Lot after Abram left and reaffirmed His promises to him, to make him the father of many children.   True/False
10. Abram was living in a tent.   True/False

GENESIS 14
POEM, PRAYERS AND DECLARATIONS

POEM
The Battle Is On

The battle is on, the battle is on
Ched-or-laomer King of Edom
The battle is on, the battle is on
King of Gomorrah, King of Sodom.

The battle is on, the battle is on
Ched-or-laomer has defeated,
Gomorrah and Sodom
Gomorrah and Sodom.

The battle is on, the battle is on
Woe to Ched-or-laomer who captured Lot
One man escaped and brought the news
Lot is captured, tell Abram the Hebrew.

The battle is on, the battle is on
Abram and his army defeated Ched-or-laomer
The battle is on, the battle is on
Lot and his people delivered by warrior Abram.

LESSON

➤   Do what you can to deliver a family member in need.
➤   Be courageous in times of battles.
➤   Seek to win your battles with godly support.
➤   Those who pick fights with God's
people will eventually be defeated.

PRAYER

Lord, help us to fight for the deliverance of our love ones
without fear and in a godly manner in Jesus name.

DECLARATION

I will fight in prayer for the deliverance of my family.
I have the strength to face the battles of life in Jesus name.

FOCUS PSALM
PSALM 14:4-5

*Have all the workers of iniquity no knowledge? Who eat
up my people as they eat bread and call not on the Lord.
There were they in great fear, for God is
in the generation of the righteous*

ADDITIONAL PRAYER POINTS AND DECLARATION BASED ON GENESIS 14

1. Lord, show me the way of escape out of every bad situation in Jesus name [14:13].
2. Lord, intervene in every warlike situation in this family/community/nation [14:21].
3. Lord, release any righteous person in bondage as Lot was released in Jesus name [14:12]
4. Lord, as I pray inform me of any member of my family/church in captivity unlawfully and free them in Jesus name.
5. Lord, do not allow anyone against me and my family have the victory over us in Jesus name [14:3].
6. God, Possessor of heaven and earth, release your blessings on us in abundance in Jesus name [14:19].
7. I receive the blessings of God in abundance in Jesus name [14:19].
8. I will fight for my family's deliverance and freedom as Abraham fought for Lot.
9. Lord, open my eyes to clearly recognize those who are for me and those who are against me in Jesus name. [14:1]
10. I declare victory over every battle in my life in Jesus name.

RELEVANT SCRIPTURE READING ON GENESIS

Hebrew 7:1-2
Hebrews 7:4, 10-22
James 4:1

GENESIS 14 QUIZ
ANSWER TRUE OR FALSE

1. Chedorlaomer was the king of Elam.   True/False
2. There was war with Chedoalomer
   and King of Sodom.   True/False
3. Bera was the king of Sodom and Birsha
   was the king of Gomorrah.   True/False
4. The valley of Siddim was full of slime pits.   True/False
5. Lot was taken captive by the king of Sodom.   True/False
6. Abram rescued Lot with 318 men.   True/False
7. Melchizedek, King of Salem was the priest
   of the Most High God.   True/False
8. Abram refused to take any goods from the
   King of Sodom.   True/False
9. Abram said that not even thread from a shoe
   latchet would he take from the King of Elam   True/False
10. Melchizedek greeted Abram by saying
    'blessed be Abram of the Most High God'.   True/False

GENESIS 15
POEM, PRAYERS AND DECLARATIONS

POEM
God Encourages Abram

The Word of the Lord came to Abram in a vision
"I am thy great reward, I am thy shield"
The Word of the Lord came to Abram in a vision
"You shall not be childless, you shall have seed.

Look to the heavens, count the stars if you can
So shall your seed be, numerous on this land".

Abram took a heifer, she-goat and ram, all three years old
Turtledove, a young pigeon to the Most High, Lord
The Word of the Lord came to Abram, "yes Abram
Your children shall be strangers and servants, in this land.

That nation shall afflict them for four hundred years
But I will judge the nations and deliver them".
The Word of the Lord came to Abram, Abram; yes Abram!

"Thou shall go to thy fathers in peace, buried in a good old age
But the fourth generation, the fourth generation,
they shall come hither again".
The Word of the Lord came to Abram,
Yes Abram, Abram, yes Abram.

LESSON

➤ God speaks to His people; allow Him to speak to you.
➤ Listen to God when He speaks.
➤ You can use something as a symbol in your life
to remind yourself of the promises of God.

GOD IN GENESIS

❖ God is a promise maker and a promise reminder- He
revealed Himself like this to Abram on numerous occasions.
❖ God is a covenant maker.
❖ God knows the future - He made Abram aware of what
will take place the next hundreds of years to his generation.

PRAYER

Lord, help me to hold on to your promises in Jesus name.

DECLARATION

I will not let go of the promises of God.

FOCUS PSALM
PSALM 15:1-2

Lord who shall abide in thy tabernacle?
Who shall dwell in thy holy hill?
He that walketh uprightly, and worketh righteousness
and speaketh the truth in his heart

ADDITIONAL PRAYER POINTS AND DECLARATIONS BASED ON GENESIS 15

1. Lord, my shield and my reward, confirm your promises to me in dreams and visions as you did to Abram in Jesus name [15:1].
2. Lord, what will you give me in my season of fruitlessness? [15:2]
3. Lord God who brought Abraham out of Ur, bless us with wealth and great inheritance, spiritual and material in Jesus name [15:7].
4. Lord, give us a glimpse of the future of our offspring and generation as you did for Abraham in Jesus name. [15:13].
5. We are blessed and free from fruitlessness.
6. I declare, I shall walk in the blessings of God.

GENESIS 15 QUIZ
ANSWER TRUE OR FALSE

1. The Word of the Lord came to Abram in a vision saying 'fear not'.   True/False
2. God told Abram to number the stars.   True/False
3. Abram believed the Lord and so he was counted as righteous.   True/False
4. God told Abram his children would be afflicted in a strange land.   True/False
5. Abram fell in a light sleep and the Lord spoke to him.   True/False
6. The Lord made a covenant with Abram to give his children land.   True/False
7. God reminded Abram that he brought him out of Ur of the Chaldees.   True/False
8. God said He would judge the nation that Abrams' children would serve.   True/False

RELEVANT SCRIPTURE READING ON GENESIS 15

Romans 4:3-6
Romans 4:20-25
Galatians 3:6
Acts 7:2-3
Hebrews 11:13
2 Peter 3:8-9

GENESIS 16
POEM, PRAYERS AND DECLARATIONS

POEM
Ismael

Ishmael, Ishmael
Ishmael came to be
A child of Abram and Hagar,
What a story.

Abram and Sarai
Just could not wait
God seemed to be taking so long
They were well up in age.

Ishmael, Ishmael
Ishmael came to be
A child of Abram and Hagar,
What a story.

Abram go to my handmaid
was Sarai's plea
Abram hearken to her
Ishmael was to be.

Hagar, Sarai's handmaid
Got pregnant soon
As Abram hearken to Sarai
Ishmael was to be.

Hagar hated Sarai
Sarai treated her harsh
Hager ran away
From Sarai, she ran fast

The angel of the Lord came
To Hagar in the wilderness
He said "Hagar whence cometh thou
Go back, go back to Sarai thy mistress.

Go back home I say
Do return, I impel
You shall bear a son
Call him Ishmael".

Ishmael, Ishmael
Ishmael came to be
A child of Abram and Hagar
What a story.

LESSONS

➢ It is best to wait on the Lord.
➢ Do not run from challenges when it's not necessary.
➢ Refuse ungodly advice.

GOD IN GENESIS.

❖ God is attentive and caring - He sent His messengers to attend to Hagar, a pregnant woman in need.
❖ God gives guidance and wise counsel - He directed Abram how to manage his household.

PRAYER

Lord, give me the wisdom and strength to reject any advice that is clearly not according to your perfect will in Jesus name. Amen

DECLARATION

I reject every ungodly advice, I will wait on the Lord.

FOCUS PSALM
PSALM 16:5

*The Lord is the portion of my inheritance
and my cup, thou maintain my lot
The lines have failed unto me in pleasant
places; yea I have a goodly heritage.*

ADDITIONAL PRAYER POINTS AND DECLARATION BASED ON GENESIS 16

1. Lord, help me in this season of fruitlessness to hold on to your promises in Jesus name [16:1].
2. I reject every evil and unwise counsel in Jesus' name[16:2].
3. I will walk in the will of the Lord.
4. Lord, forgive me of all the wrongs I have done in Jesus name [16:5].
5. Lord, in times of hardship and persecution, give me strength to stand in Jesus name [16:6].
6. Lord, show me how to deal with persons who treat me in an unfair and harsh manner in Jesus name [16:6].
7. I will boldly face the challenges of life with God's help in Jesus name.
8. Lord, send ministering angels to minister to us in our times of weakness in Jesus name [16:7-11].
9. I will call on the name of the Lord; He hears and speaks to His people [16:13].
10. Thank you Lord for those persons you sent into my life to give me godly advice.

RELEVANT SCRIPTURE READING ON GENESIS 16

Galatians 4:20-25
1 Peter 3:7

GENESIS 16 QUIZ
ANSWER TRUE OR FALSE

1. Sarai was Hagar's sister.   True/False
2. Sarai gave Hager to her husband so that he
    could be a father of a child.   True/False
3. When Hagar conceived she loved Sarai more.   True/False
4. Sarah regretted giving Tamar to Abram so
    he could have children.   True/False
5. Sarah fled from Hagar when she became pregnant. True/False
6. Hagar told the serpent she was running
    from Abram.   True/False
7. An angel told Hagar to return home and
    submit to Sarai.   True/False
8. The angel of the Lord said Ishmael would
    be a wild man.   True/False
9. Hagar called the name of the Lord 'Thou God
    that sees me'.   True/False
10. Abram was 86 years old when Ishmael was born. True/False

GENESIS 17:1-14, 23-27
POEM, PRAYERS AND DECLARATIONS

POEM
Father Of Nations

Father of nations, Abram's name changed
Again God remind him of the covenant He made
"I will multiply thee and make thee great
You are no longer Abram, there is a name change.

You shall be fruitful, I will make of thee nations and kings
I will establish my covenant between thee, thy seed and me.

Father of nations, Abram's name changed.
Again God reminded Abraham of the covenant He made.

"Circumcise every male child eight years old
Circumcision, a sign of our covenant for evermore".
So Abraham took every male child and circumcised
Abraham was circumcised ninety years old and nine.

LESSON

➢ Circumcise your heart to God.

GOD IN GENESIS

❖ God will remind you of His promises
as He reminded Abram.

❖ God has the power and resources to bless you
beyond measure.- as He blessed Abram.

❖ God is Almighty – when He appeared unto
Abram He said 'I am the Almighty God'.

❖ God is revelational – He revealed Himself to Abram.

❖ God is understanding – He understood Abram's
plight of fatherlessness and comforted him.

PRAYER

Lord, help me not to forget your promises
to me in Jesus name. Amen

DECLARATION

The Lord is reminding me of His promises.
I will not forget the promises of God.

FOCUS PSALM
PSALM 17:7-8

7 Shew thy marvelous lovingkindness, O thou that
savest by thy right hand them which put their trust
in thee from those that rise up against them.
8 Keep me as the apple of the eye, hide me
under the shadow of thy wings,

ADDITIONAL PRAYER POINTS AND DECLARATIONS BASED ON GENESIS 17

1. Thank you Lord for your presence, I will walk before you in righteousness [17:1].
2. Lord, I bow in worship to you [16:3].
3. The Lord will make me and my family productive and fruitful [17:6].
4. My family members will be good leaders in Jesus name [17:6].
5. Lord, demonstrate yourself as God in my life and circumstances [17:8].
6. Lord, thank you for the covenant you made with Abraham. I shall walk in those covenant blessings [17:8].
7. Circumcise my heart Lord to total commitment and service in your kingdom in Jesus name [17:11].
8. Bless us Lord as you blessed Sarai.
9. The blessing of the Lord is upon me and my family [17:6-8].
10. I will hold on to the everlasting covenant and promises of God [17:13].

GENESIS 17 QUIZ
ANSWER TRUE OR FALSE

1. Abram fell on his back and talked with God.   True/False
2. God said he would not keep his covenant with
   Abram's generation.   True/False
3. God said 'every male child in Abram's
   family was to be circumcised.   True/False
4. Abram's name was changed to Abraham and
   Sarai to Sarah.   True/False
5. At 98 years old Abraham was circumcised.   True/False
6. God said every male child in Abraham's
   life was to be circumcised.   True/False
7. God said he would bless Sarah to be the
   mother of only one nation.   True/False
8. God said he would not make Ishmael
   great only Isaac, Abraham's son.   True/False
9. Abraham circumcised Ishmael and the
   other women in his house.   True/False
10. God said every boy child in Abram's house eight
    days old and older should to be circumcised.   True/False

GENESIS 17:15-27, 18:12-15
POEM, PRAYERS AND DECLARATIONS

POEM
They Laughed

It's not a joke, but Abraham laughed
Fell on his face and said in his heart
Ha, ha, ha, shall a child be born in my old age
Shall Sarah give birth in her life at this stage?

Ha, ha, ha, but it's not a joke
Ha, ha, ha, but it's not a joke
Abraham said " Lord remember I have Ishmael".
"Yes" God said, "but Sarah shall have
a child this time next year".

It's not a joke but Sarah laughed
"After I am waxed old, shall I bear a son, Ha, ha, ha?"
"Is anything too hard for me"? God asked
Yes you shall have a son, ha, ha, ha

Sarah denied laughing, God said "yes you did"
"But you shall have a child next year"; no joke, it's no kid

Ha, ha, ha, ha, ha, ha!
Ha, ha, ha, ha, ha, ha!

LESSON

> ➢ Even when we laugh God notices.
> ➢ Impossible things are possible with God.

GOD IN GENESIS

❖ God is able to do the impossible in your life.
❖ God's plan and promises at times may seem ridiculous and like a joke but believe and expect it to come to pass.
❖ God communicates with His people in different ways.
❖ God is sympathetic to His people - In Abraham's old age He again reminded him of His promises to him.

PRAYER

Heavenly Father, take away any and every reservations I have regarding Your promises to me Jesus name.

DECLARATION

I will see the promises of God come to pass in my life.

FOCUS PSALM
PSALM 17:7-8

7 Shew thy marvelous lovingkindness, O thou that savest by thy right hand them which put their trust in thee from those that rise up against them. 8 Keep me as the apple of the eye, hide me under the shadow of thy wings,

ADDITIONAL PRAYER POINTS AND DECLARATIONS BASED ON GENESIS 17

1. Praise the Lord for his wonderful promises to me [17:17].
2. I will rejoice in the Lord for His amazing promises to me [17:17].
3. Lord, help the children in our family to live a righteous life before you in Jesus name [17:18].
4. Lord, establish the Abrahamic covenant in my life and family in Jesus name [17:19].
5. Praise be to God who hears my prayer [17:20].
6. I declare the blessing of God is on my life [17:20].
7. I praise you Lord for the awesome things you will do in my life [17:17]
8. I will not laugh at things that seem impossible to me, for all things are possible with God [17:20].
9. I rejoice in the Lord my God.
10. Lord God as I go out today, go with me, in Jesus name [17:22].
11. Lord, I circumcise my heart to you; I recommit my life to you, to serve you wholeheartedly in Jesus name [17:23].

RELEVANT SCRIPTURE READING ON GENESIS 17

Romans 9:7-9

Galatians 4;28-31

Galatians 3:16

1 Peter 3:6

Romans 2:25

GENESIS 17 QUIZ

Fill in the blank spaces with the correct words below

Ishmael, Isaac, circumcised, covenant, Sarah, face,

1. But my _____ will I establish with Isaac which Sarah shall bear unto thee.
2. Abraham fell on his _____ and laughed.
3. And God said, _____ thy wife shall bear thee a son and thou shall call his name _____.
4. And _____ was thirteen years old when he was circumcised.
5. Abraham and Ishmael was _____ the same day.

GENESIS 18
POEM, PRAYERS AND DECLARATIONS

POEM
Abraham And The Guests

The Lord appeared to Abraham in the plains of Mamre
Abraham lifted up his eyes and lo three men
Immediately Abraham ran to met them at the tent door
Solemnly bowed himself, yes bowed towards the floor.

"My Lord", Abraham said, "if I have found favor in thy sight
I pray from thy servant do not just pass by
Allow us to entertain you, I'll fetch a morsel of bread
Stay, make yourself comfortable, rest
The meal, I will fetch".

Abraham and Sarah together prepared a meal
Meal of butter, cake, milk and beef
"Where is Sarah thy wife?" one of the three men asked.
"Sarah shall have a son this time next year when I pass".

LESSON

> ➤ Be hospitable to others.
> ➤ It's good when a husband and wife work in unity even in unexpected circumstances.
> ➤ Let us seek to entertain the presence of God in our lives.

PRAYER

Lord, help me to be more hospitable and a
better host when persons visit my home.

DECLARATION

I will entertain the presence of God through worship and prayer.

FOCUS PSALM
PSALM 18:46

*The Lord liveth; and blessed be my rock; and
let the God of my salvation be exalted.*

ADDITIONAL PRAYER POINTS AND DECLARATIONS BASED ON GENESIS 18

1. I acknowledge the presence of the Lord in this place [18;1].
2. Lord, show yourself and let your presence be evident in my life [18:1].
3. Even when the days are hot I will commune with God [18:1].
4. Lord, open my eyes to see spiritual things as I worship you [18:2].
5. Lord, do not pass me by if I have found favour in your sight [18:3].

6. Lord, abide with me in this place [18:4].
7. Lord, let every husband/wife be aware of their spouse's spiritual whereabouts and level with you [18:9].
8. Even in old age I will experience happiness and joy [18:12].
9. Blessed be the Lord for nothing is too hard for Him [18:14].
10. God will work wonders in my life at the appointed time [18:14].

GENESIS 18 QUIZ
ANSWER TRUE OR FALSE

1. The Lord appeared to Abraham in the plains of Mamre.   True/False
2. Abraham asked the visitors to wash their hands and feet before they ate the food.   True/False
3. Abraham was told that his wife would not bear children.   True/False
4. Sarah denied that she laughed because she was afraid.   True/False
5. Abraham gave his visitors cake and milk to eat.   True/False
6. Sarah asked if the Lord would destroy Sodom even if they found fifty righteous.   True/False
7. Abraham described himself as dust and ashes.   True/False
8. Abraham did not know where Sarah was when God asked for her.   True/False
9. Sarah laughed at the thought of having a child in her old age.   True/False
10. Sarah admitted that she laughed because she was afraid.   True/False

GENESIS 18:17-33
POEM, PRAYERS AND DECLARATIONS

POEM
Abraham's Plea

The Lord asked, 'shall I hide from Abraham
what I shall do to Sodom'
"No" says the Lord, 'I will tell him, for he
shall become a great and mighty nation
The cry of Sodom and Gomorrah is great,
I will destroy that city Sodom,
city of the unrighteous".

Abraham asked "Lord will you destroy the
righteous ones with the wickedly
Peradventure there be fifty righteous
will you still destroy the city
That be far from thee to do after this manner
To slay the righteous with the wicked thou mighty Banner.

The righteous judged as the wicked that be far from my King
Shall not the Judge of the all the earth do the right thing"
The Lord replied, "If I find in Sodom fifty righteous within
I will spare the entire city for their sake, yes I will"

"Lord, peradventure only forty-five righteous are there
Would you still destroy the city", Abraham declared
"No, my son, for the sake of forty
righteous one I will not destroy
Neither will I destroy if thirty or twenty are found".

"But Lord what if there is only ten righteous
in the city", Abraham queried
"No", says the Lord, "I will not destroy the
city if only ten righteous dwell"
After they communicated, the Lord went his way
While Abraham, father of nations return to his place.

LESSON

> ➢ There is a time for everything, a time for mercy and a time for judgment.
> ➢ Prayer plays a key role in the deliverance of God's people from national judgement.

GOD IN GENESIS

> ❖ God is merciful - He exercised His mercy towards the righteous even in times of judgment.
> ❖ God is a good listener - He carefully and patiently listened to Abraham's pleas.

PRAYER

Lord, make me a better intercessor.

DECLARATION

God has heard my cry.

FOCUS PSALM
PSALM 18:13-14

13 The Lord also thundered in the heavens, and the Highest gave his voice; hailstones and coals of fire. 14 Yea, he sent out his arrows, and scattered them; and he shot out lightings, and discomfited them

ADDITIONAL PRAYER POINTS AND DECLARATIONS BASED ON GENESIS 18

1. Lord, help me to walk with you every step that I take in Jesus name [18:11].
2. Lord, in Jesus name reveal to me the things that are necessary for me to know, by your grace [18:17].
3. Lord, in Jesus name, help the parents in our families to guide their children in the way of the Lord [18:19].
4. We shall keep the way of the Lord to do justice [18:19].
5. Lord, have mercy on this nation, spare it, for the righteous sake in Jesus name [18:20].
6. O Heavenly Father, search us, examine us and have mercy in our times of rebellion and sin in Jesus name [18:21].
7. Lord, I pray that you preserve the righteous among the wicked in times of judgment in Jesus name [18:23].
8. Lord, withhold your wrath and spare this city for the sake of the righteous in Jesus name [18:24].
9. I declare that the mercies of God be extended on this nation in Jesus name [18:24].
10. I will continue to intercede for this nation/family by the grace of God in Jesus name.

RELEVANT SCRIPTURE READING ON GENESIS 18

Acts 7:2

Hebrews 13:2

1 Peter 4:4

Romans 9:9

Romans 4:19-21

Galatians 3:8-9

GENESIS 18 QUIZ

Complete the following verses with the appropriate words below.

angry, wicked, cry, judgment, Lord, hide, great, mighty, commune righteous, Sodom

1. Shall I _____ from Abraham that thing which I do.
2. And the men rose up and looked towards _____.
3. Abraham shall surely become a great and _____ nation.
4. They shall keep the way of the Lord to do _____ and judgment.
5. Behold the _____ of Sodom and Gomorrah is _____ because their sin is very grievous.
6. Abraham stood before the _____.
7. Wilt thou destroy the righteous with the _____.
8. If I find fifty _____ I will spare all the place for their sakes.
9. Oh let not the Lord be _____ and I will speak
10. And the Lord went his way as soon as he left _____ with Abraham.

GENESIS 19
POEM, PRAYERS AND DECLARATIONS

POEM
Sodom And Gomorrah Is No More

Sodom and Gomorrah is no more
Sodom and Gomorrah is no more
Listen how this came about
Sodom and Gomorrah is no more.

At evening two angels came to the city of Sodom
At Sodom's gate Lot met them, with
bowed face towards the ground
"Come to my place" Lot pleaded "and do tarry all night
Wash your feet and go your way early morning bright".

They entered Lot's house and had a feast
Baked unleavened bread they all did eat

Sodom and Gomorrah is destroyed
Sodom and Gomorrah is destroyed
Listen how this came about
Sodom and Gomorrah is destroyed.

The men of Sodom came, before Lot's guess laid down
Both young and old men came from all around.
"Where are the men that came to see thee tonight?
'Bring them out to us", demand the Sodomites.

"Don't do this wickedness", Lot pleaded;
he hurried to shut the door
"I will give you my two daughters to know, they are pure"
"Give us those men" demanded the Sodomites
"Give us those men to know, we want them tonight".

Bam, Bam, bam, bam, on the door the Sodomites pressed
In a moment both small and great Sodomites
were struck with blindness
Bam, Bam, bam, bam, on the door the Sodomites pressed
In a moment both small and great Sodomites
were struck with blindness.

Sodom and Gomorrah is destroyed
Sodom and Gomorrah is destroyed
Listen how this came about
Sodom and Gomorrah is destroyed.

"Lot, take your family and go, we will destroy this place".
The angels said, "take your family and
go, for Sodom's sin is great"
Lot summoned his family saying 'let's go from this place
The city will be destroyed, its sin is great'.

"Quickly, escape for thy life" the angels plea
"Take your two daughters and wife hurriedly".
The angels' plea, "Lot, make haste and do not look back".
Lot and family made haste, made haste to the city of Zoar

Woe, woe, Lot's wife look back and turn a salt pillar
Fire and brimstone rained and destroyed
the cities Sodom and Gomorrah

Woe, woe, Lot's wife look back and turn a salt pillar
Fire and brimstone rained and destroyed
the cities Sodom and Gomorrah.

Sodom and Gomorrah is destroyed
Woe Sodom and Gomorrah is destroyed
Sodom and Gomorrah is destroyed
Woe Sodom and Gomorrah is destroyed.

LESSON

➢ It is best to move quickly as God directs
you and avoid procrastination.
➢ Looking back at your old ungodly way of life
with a longing to return can be detrimental.
➢ Deliverance comes at the time we need it most.
➢ Sin still pervades the earth but God will judge.

GOD IN GENESIS

❖ God is judge- He judged the wicked
people of Sodom and Gomorrah
❖ God is a deliverer - He delivered His people.
❖ God is caring - He warned and guided
His people to places of safety.

PRAYER

Lord may I move at your command and work with
your plan of deliverance in Jesus name. Amen

DECLARATION

God has a plan, He will deliver me.

FOCUS PSALM
PSALM 19:9

*The fear of the Lord is clean, enduring forever: the
judgments of the Lord are true and righteous altogether.*

ADDITIONAL PRAYER POINTS AND DECLARATIONS FOR GENESIS BASED ON 19

1. Lord, I bow my heart in worship to you, for your worthy to be praised [19:1].
2. Lord, help me to stand guard at the spiritual gate of our house and family in Jesus name [19:1].
3. Lord, deliver us from the troubles that come to our house in Jesus name [19:4].
4. Lord, those whom you send to visit us, let no harm come to them in Jesus name [19:5-8].
5. Lord, lift us/our family out of a place of sinfulness and wickedness in Jesus name [19:12].
6. Lord, in Jesus name, guard and protect me and my household from all evil [19:4].
7. Lord, protect the daughters in our families from the unwise decisions of their parents/love ones [19:8].
8. Lord, protect our children from all sexual, emotional and psychological abuse in the name of Jesus Christ [19:8].
9. Lord, protect us from the evil elements of society [19:8].
10. Lord, cause the unsaved to run for their lives to the Rock, the Lord Jesus Christ [19:17].
11. I declare, we will not turn back or look back to a life of sinfulness in Jesus name [19:11].
12. The Lord will come to our rescue and deliver us with His mighty hand [19:9].

GENESIS 19 QUIZ

Complete the following verse with the appropriate words below

remembered, blindness, two, pulled, door, house, pillar, brimstone, furnace, risen, know, look,

1. Bring them out unto us that we may _____ them.
2. Behold I have _____ daughters which have not known man.
3. The men put forth their hand and _____ Lot in to the _____.
4. They smote the men that were at the _____ of the house with _____.
5. The Lord rained upon Sodom and Gomorrah _____ and fire out of heaven.
6. Escape for thy life _____ not behind thee.
7. His wife looked back behind him and she became a _____ salt.
8. The sun was _____ upon the earth when _____ entered Zoar.
9. The smoke of the country went up as the smoke of a _____.
10. When God destroyed the cities of the plain God_____ Abraham.

GENESIS 19: 31-38
POEM, PRAYERS AND DECLARATIONS

POEM
It Is Forbidden

Our father is old, no other man on earth
Let's mate with him my sister, of children give birth
'Come, my sister'. Lot's daughter says, 'it's just us two
Let's mate with our father and have children soon'.

It's forbidden, I say, 'It's forbidden
It's forbidden I say it's forbidden

The firstborn daughter said to the younger,
"let's make our father drunk tonight
We will lie with him, both of us as he would a wife".
It's forbidden I say it's forbidden
It's forbidden I say it's forbidden.

Both daughters got pregnant and had their child
The first born had a son called father of the Moabites
The younger daughter had a son, Benaomi was his name
Benaomi, the father of the children of Amman to this day.

It's forbidden I say it's forbidden
What these daughters did
It's forbidden I say it's forbidden
What these daughters did.

LESSON

- ➤ Avoid strong drink else you may get drunk.
- ➤ Wait on the Lord for a life's partner.
- ➤ Refuse to do anything that is forbidden by God.
- ➤ Reject evil counsel.
- ➤ Sometime it's the person we trust that seek to do us harm. so put your complete trust in God.

PRAYER

Lord, help our sisters in the Lord to resist the temptation to purposefully have a child out of wedlock because they have not gotten a husband as yet.

DECLARATION

I refuse to get involved in things forbidden by God.

FOCUS PSALM

Psalm 19:12-13
12 Who can understand his errors? cleanse thou me from secret faults.
13 Keep back thy servant also from presumptuous sins; let them not have dominion over me: then shall I be upright, and I shall be innocent from the great transgression.

ADDITIONAL PRAYERS AND DECLARATIONS BASED ON GENESIS 19

1. Lord, let your presence be a shelter for me and my family in the name of Jesus Christ [19:30].
2. Lord take away any fear I may have that's not of you, in the name of Jesus Christ [19:30].
3. I will not live in fear in the name of Jesus Christ [19:30].
4. I reject and dispel every fear from my life in the name of Jesus Christ.
5. Lord, I commit every firstborn child to you in this family, may they live holy lives and give good counsel in the name of Jesus Christ.
6. Lord, help us to recognize and reject any unwise counsel, in the name of Jesus Christ [19:31].
7. I reject any evil counsel in the name of Jesus Christ. [19:31].
8. Lord, any person planning to do us harm and wrong, expose it to me now, in the name of Jesus Christ [19:33].
9. Lord, protect and shield me from the wicked plans of those against me, in Jesus name [19:33].
10. Lord, have mercy and forgive those of us who have walked contrary to your way, in Jesus name [19:33].
11. Lord, I pray for those among us who were born in unfortunate circumstances, may you deliver them from the consequences of their parents' sins and wicked deeds in Jesus name [19:37].
12. I declare that I will walk in the wisdom and counsel of God in Jesus name.

RELEVANT SCRIPTURE READING ON

2 Peter 2:7-9

Jude 7

2 Peter 2:6

Amos 4:11

GENESIS 19 QUIZ

Read Chapter and Fill in the blanks

Ammon, father, earth, Moab, Benammi, Moabites, mountains, perceive, wine, daughters

1. Lot went out of Zoar and dwelt in the _____.
2. He dwelt in a cave he and his _____.
3. Both daughters of Lot were with child by their _____.
4. The younger arose and lay with him and he _____ not when she lay down.
5. They made their father drink _____ that night.
6. Our father is old there is not a man in the _____ to come in.
7. Benammi is the father of the children of _____.
8. The firstborn bear a son called his name _____.
9. Moab is the father of the _____.
10. The younger called her son _____.

GENESIS 20
POEM, PRAYERS AND DECLARATIONS

Restore His Wife

Restore the man, his wife
Restore the man, his wife
She is not his sister as he declared
She is his wife, his wife,

Abraham journeyed to Gerar with his wife
Introduced her to king Abimelech, as
his sister not partner for life
God dreamed Abimelech that night, saying,
"behold you're a dead man
For you have in your possession Sarah, the wife of Abraham".

God said "Abimelech you're a man of integrity of heart
I kept you from touching her that was my part
Restore the mans, his wife for he is a prophet of mine
Then Abraham shall pray for you, and you shall live, not die.

If you do not restore her, you will not live
You will die and everything that is
yours if you refuse to do this".
Abimelech arose and told these things to his servants and men
Summoned Abraham and queried why he did such offence

"Sarah is your wife, you deceived me my friend
Why did you do this, you did I offend?"
"No" said Abraham, "I was just afraid
I thought surely the fear of God is not in this place".

Abimelech returned Sarah, Abraham's wife with sheep and oxen
Thousand pieces of silver with servants, both men and women
Abimelech and his wife got healed as Abraham prayed
Closed wombs opened, of his wife and his maids.

Restore the man, his wife
Restore the man, his wife
She is not his sister as he declared
She is his wife, his wife, his wife!

LESSON

- ➤ God fights for marriages.
- ➤ It is better to speak the truth for your sake and others.
- ➤ Protect and honor your spouse.
- ➤ God tends to warn people before He sends judgment.

GOD IN GENESIS

- ❖ God is our protector - He stepped in the situation and protected Sarah and also Abimelech in his ignorance.
- ❖ God is a loving and just God- He warned Abimelech of an impending judgment because of his possession of Sarah.

PRAYER

Lord, cause us to experience a restoration
of marital/family blessings.

DECLARATION

I will honour and protect my love ones/spouse

FOCUS PSALM
PSALM 20:6

Now know I that the Lord saveth his anointed; he will hear him from his holy heaven with the saving strength of his right hand.

ADDITIONAL PRAYER POINTS AND DECLARATIONS BASED ON GENESIS 20

1. Lord, as I journey to a new place today, go with me in the name of Jesus Christ.
2. Lord, speak to the enemies of my family and terminate their plan to harm us in Jesus name [20:2].
3. Lord, restore the blessings that were taken away from us in Jesus name [20:7].
4. Lord, remember those who have deceived me, let the truth be revealed [20:9].
5. I speak healing to those who are hurting in the name of Jesus.
6. Lord, keep me from sinning against you and help me be a person of integrity in Jesus name [20:6].
7. I declare I will walk in righteousness and integrity [20:6].
8. Lord, help me to wake up and start my day early to do the things that are necessary for the day in Jesus name. [20:8].
9. Lord, may we take your warning seriously and act quickly to avert judgment as a nation [20:8].
10. Lord, in Jesus name forgive me if I have judged anyone wrongfully and help me to see people through your eyes [20:11].
11. Lord, I commit my wife/husband to you, for your protection, guidance and preservation in Jesus name [20:12].
12. Lord as Abraham prayed so I pray that you heal the persons we have offended and hurt, in Jesus name [20:18].

RELEVANT SCRIPTURE READING

Colossian 3:9

GENESIS 20 QUIZ
ANSWER TRUE OR FALSE

1. Abraham said Sarah was his cousin.   True/False
2. God came to Abimelech in a dream by night.   True/False
3. Abraham feared that God would kill him
    because of his wife's beauty.   True/False
4. Abraham admitted to Abimelech that Sarah was
    the daughter of his father who became his wife.   True/False
5. Abimelech ask if God would slay a
    righteous nation.   True/False
6. God told Abimelech to return Sarai to Abraham
    else he would die.   True/False
7. Abimelech told Sarah that he gave her brother
    one thousand pieces of silver.   True/False
8. God described Abraham as a prophet and king.   True/False
9. Abraham thought the fear of God was not in Gerar.   True/False
10. Abraham gave his wife back to Abimelech
    with oxen and sheep.   True/False

GENESIS 21
POEM, PRAYERS AND DECLARATIONS

POEM
Halleluyah, Sarah Bears A Son

In her old age Sarah had a son
At one hundred year's old Abrahams' son Isaac was born
Abraham circumcised him eight days later
Son of his old age, answer to prayer
Hallelujah, hallelujah Sarah conceived and bears a son
In her old age, yes in her old age, it was done.

Same day Isaac was weaned, Abraham had a feast
Sarah saw Ishmael, son of Hagar, the Egyptian mocking him
Sarah said "Abraham cast out this bond woman and her son
For the son of this bond woman shall not be heir with my son".

The thing grieved Abraham but God said "let Ishmael go
For in Isaac your inheritance shall be, Isaac alone".

LESSON

> God keeps his promises.
> It's good to celebrate the growth stages of our lives
> Take your family issues to the Lord in prayer

GOD IN GENESIS

❖ God is a promise giver and keeper- His promise to Abraham and Sarah came to pass.
❖ God is wise - He instructed Abraham to do what was best for the family.

PRAYER

Lord, thank you for every promise you have made to me and caused it to come to pass.

DECLARATION

The promises of God will come to pass.

FOCUS PSALM
PSALM 21:1-2

The king shall joy in thy strength, O Lord; and in
thy salvation how greatly shall he rejoice!
2 Thou hast given him his heart's desire, and hast
not withholden the request of his lips. Selah.

ADDITIONAL PRAYERS AND DECLARATIONS BASED ON GENESIS 21

1. Lord, visit me and let Your presence be evident in my life in Jesus name [21:1].
2. Lord, visit me and fulfill your promises in my life in Jesus name [21:1].
3. Lord, visit me and help me to handle any difficult situation in my life [21:1].
4. Lord, may I conceive and bare (spiritual) children for the kingdom of God in Jesus name. [21:2].
5. God made me laugh and rejoice, halleluiah! [21:6]
6. Lord, bless us so that we can have regular family feast and gathering in Jesus name [21:8].
7. Lord, in Jesus name do mighty things among us and give us added reasons to rejoice and celebrate [21:8].
8. I rejoice in the Lord [21:8].
9. Lord, I commit every grievous situation to you, fix it in the name of Jesus Christ [21:11].
10. I will arise early in the morning and do what the Lord commands in Jesus name [21:12].

GENESIS 21 QUIZ
ANSWER TRUE OR FALSE

1. Abraham circumcised Isaac when he was eight years old.   True/False
2. Abraham was 98 years old when Isaac was born. True/False
3. Abraham made a great feast the same day Isaac was weaned.   True/False
4. Sarah saw Ishmael mocking his older brother Isaac.   True/False
5. Sarah said 'God made me to laugh'.   True/False
6. Sarah told Abraham to cast out Hagar and Ishmael. True/False

7. Abraham was happy when Sarah told him to
   cast out the bond woman's son.   True/False
8. Early in the morning Abraham rose up and
   gave Hagar bread and water.   True/False
9. God agreed with Sarah that the bond woman
   and her son should leave.   True/False
10. Sarah wandered in the wilderness of Beersheba.   True/False

GENESIS 21:14-20
POEM, PRAYERS AND DECLARATIONS

POEM
Hagar And Son

Abraham rose early morning, gave Hagar water and bread
To the wilderness of Beersheba, Hagar and Ishmael fled.
After drinking the last of the water, Hagar
hid Ishmael under the shrubs
Lifted her voice and wept, wept wept, wept for her son.

God heard the child's voice and the angel called out
"Hagar, what's wrong, fear not, God has heard your child voice
Arise, lift up your son, hold him in your hand
I will make your son Ishmael a great nation".

God opened Hagar's eyes, a well of water she saw
Their thirst was quenched; Ishmael grew and became an archer.

LESSON

> ➢ God hears the cries of his children.
> ➢ Even in the wilderness the Lord provides.
> ➢ God is everlasting

PRAYER

Lord, hear the voice of the children in our family
and community and save them, in Jesus name.

DECLARATION

God is my provider.

FOCUS PSALM

Psalm 21:4
*He asked life of thee, and thou gavest it him,
even length of days forever and ever.*

ADDITIONAL PRAYER POINTS AND DECLARATIONS BASED ON GENESIS 21

1. Lord, give me the strength to put away anything in my life that is not of you [21:14].
2. Lord, fill my cupboard and fridge with bread and water, with all that is needed for daily nutritional meals in Jesus name [21:14].
3. I reject depression and discouragement in the name of Jesus. I will not give up on life in the name of Jesus [21:15-16].
4. Hear my cry Lord, see my tears, come and deliver in the name of Jesus [21:16].

5. I will not fear, for God is with me [21:17].
6. God, hear the cries of our children and bring deliverance [21:17].
7. Lord, open my eyes to see your goodness and favour in Jesus name [21:19].
8. Open my eyes O Lord to see the way of escape and deliverance that you have made in Jesus name [21:20].
9. God is with me even in the wilderness experiences [21:20].
10. Deliver me Lord from a season of dryness in Jesus name [21:20].

RELEVANT SCRIPTURE READING ON GENESIS

Hebrews 11:11
James 2:21
Galatians 4:30

HAGAR AND ISHMAEL IN OTHER BOOKS OF THE BIBLE

Galatians 4:25-30

GENESIS 21 QUIZ
ANSWER TRUE OF FALSE

1. When the water was finished Hagar put her son under the sycamore tree.   True/False
2. Hagar thought her son was going to die in the wilderness.   True/False
3. An angel of the Lord covered Hagar with a sheet. True/False
4. The angel said God heard Hagar's son's voice.   True/False
5. God opened Hagar's eyes and she saw a well of water.   True/False

6. Ishmael lived in Paran and Hagar gave him
    a wife from Egypt.   True/False
7. Ishmael grew up and became an archer.   True/False
8. Abimelech servants had violently taken a well.   True/False
9. Abraham and Abimelech made a covenant
    at Beersheba.   True/False
10. Abraham planted a grove in Beersheba and
    called on the name of the everlasting God.   True/False

GENESIS 22
POEM, PRAYERS AND DECLARATIONS

POEM
A Father's Sacrifice

God said "Abraham take your son Isaac
Offer him as a burnt offering in the land of Moriah".
Abraham rose up early in the morning, saddled his ass
Took two young men with him and his son Isaac.

On the third day of the journey, Abraham saw the place afar
"Abide here" Abraham told the men,
"Isaac and I will go onward".
Abraham took the wood of the burnt offering
and laid it on the young man
Grabbed both fire and knife together in his hand.

Isaac said, "Father I see the wood and
fire but where is the sacrifice"?
Abraham answered "my son my son the Lord will provide".
Abraham built the altar, on which Isaac he bound
Abraham took the knife to slay Isaac, his own son.

At that moment the angel of the Lord loudly cried out
"Abraham, Abraham, let the boy alone", he shouts.
Abraham behold a ram in the thicket caught by the horn
He offered it as a burnt offering instead of his dear son.

Jehovah Jireh, Jehovah Jireh, that Abraham named the place
A ram instead of his son, provided by God's grace
Jehovah Jireh, Jehovah Jireh, that Abraham named the place.
A ram instead of his son, provided by God's grace!

LESSON

➤ Our love for God must be more than our love for others.
➤ It is important to know the voice of God.

GOD IN GENESIS

❖ God is an examiner – At times He tests His people.
❖ God is a provider – He provided for
his people, he is our Jehovah Jireh.
❖ God will provide.

PRAYER

Lord, help me to love you more, more than
anything and anyone in this world.

DECLARATION

I will seek to know God more through
prayer and reading His Word.
I love the Lord with all my heart.

FOCUS PSALM
PSALM 22:3-5

3 But thou art holy, O thou that inhabitest the praises of Israel.
4 Our fathers trusted in thee: they trusted,
and thou didst deliver them.
5 They cried unto thee, and were delivered: they
trusted in thee, and were not confounded.

ADDITIONAL PRAYER POINTS AND DECLARATIONS OF GENESIS 22

1. Lord God, lead me not into temptation I pray, in the name of Jesus Christ [22:1].
2. Lord, teach me to know your voice as Abraham knew your voice in the name of Jesus Christ [22:2].
3. I will listen to the Lord when He speaks to me [22:2].
4. I will arise early and worship God [22:3].
5. The Lord who provided for Abraham will provide for us [22:8].
6. Lord God, Jehovah Jireh, make yourself evident in my life, provide my daily needs in the name of Jesus Christ [22:14].
7. I will walk in the blessings of Abraham, God will bless us and our family [22:17].
8. I worship you Lord and give you praise; help me to live a life of total worship to you in Jesus name [22:5].
9. Lord, strengthen the relationship we have with our parents and love ones in the name of Jesus Christ [22:7].
10. I pray that the fathers and sons in our family will build a better relationship with each other to the glory of God [22:7].

RELEVANT SCRIPTURE READING ON GENESIS

Hebrew 11:17-19
Hebrews 6:13

GENESIS 22 QUIZ
ANSWER TRUE OR FALSE

1. God told Abraham to offer his son on Mount Sinai as a burnt offering.   True/False
2. Abraham got up late the morning to take Isaac to present him as a burnt offering.   True/False

3. Abraham took an axe to slay Ishmael, his son.   True/False
4. Isaac asked his father 'where is the
    lamb for a burnt offering'.   True/False
5. Abraham told Isaac that the Lord will provide
    a ram for a burnt offering.   True/False
6. Abraham bound Isaac on the altar he
    built to offer him as sacrifice to God.   True/False
7. An angel of the Lord called out to Abraham
    to stop him from offering his son as a sacrifice.   True/False
8. Abraham saw a ram in the thicket and
    offered it instead of his wife for a sacrifice.   True/False
9. Nahor Abraham's brother had two sons,
    Huz and Buz.   True/False
10. Abraham called the place he was to slay
    his son, Jehovah Jireh.   True/False

GENESIS 23
POEM, PRAYERS AND DECLARATIONS

POEM
Death And Burial Of Sarah

"O Sarah, O Sarah", Abraham wept
"My wife Sarah has departed from me".
Sarah died at a hundred and twenty seven years old
These were the years of Sarah, Abraham's spouse.

Abraham a pilgrim needs a place to bury his wife
"A piece of land with a cave, I'll give' said Ephraim the Hittite
Abraham said 'Oh no, no Ephraim, for this land I want to pay
I will give thee money for the field with the cave".

For the property Abraham paid four hundred shekels of silver
In the cave of Machpelah, he buried his wife Sarah.

LESSON

> ➤ We may face the death of a love one, one day.
> ➤ A long life with health and strength is a blessing from God, as Sarah lived for 127 years.

PRAYER.

Lord, help us to remember and bring comfort to those who are going through times of grief.

FOCUS PSALM
PSALM 23:4

Yea, though I walk through the valley of the shadow of death, I will fear no evil: for thou art with me; thy rod and thy staff they comfort me.

ADDITIONAL PRAYER POINTS AND DECLARATIONS BASED ON GENESIS 23

1. Lord, bless us with good health and long life as you did Sarah [23:1].
2. Lord, remember those who have lost loved ones among us and bring comfort to their hearts [23:2].
3. Lord, provide sufficient funds and a proper place for burying the dead in Jesus name [23:4].
4. Lord, thank you for the support and comfort you provided for us/others who have lost loved ones.
5. I choose to be strong in difficult situations [23:6].
6. Lord, thank you for the persons you have placed among us to help in times of loss and grief [23:9].

GENESIS 23 QUIZ
ANSWER TRUE OR FALSE

1. Sarah died at 127 years old.   True/False
2. Sarah died in Kirjatharba otherwise called Hebron.   True/False
3. Abraham did not mourn for Sarah his wife.   True/False
4. Abraham bought the cave of Machpelah to bury
   his wife.   True/False
5. Ephron gave Abraham a piece of land to
   do farming.   True/False
6. The children of Heth called Abraham a
   mighty prince.   True/False
7. Abraham refused to accept the burial place
   as a gift, instead he insisted on paying for it.   True/False
8. Abraham described himself as a stranger
   among the children of Canaan.   True/False
9. Abraham bought the field of Ephron for
   400 shekels of silver.   True/False
10. The sons of Seth sold Abraham a land
   for a burying place.   True/False

GENESIS 24
POEM, PRAYERS AND DECLARATIONS

POEM
A Wife Chosen

Abraham eldest servant mandated to find Isaac a wife
A good woman, not from the daughters of the Canaanites
On a journey he set out, to find such a woman
Travelling with ten camels and goods from his master Abraham.

At a well in Mesopotamia, the servant arrived
There he met Rebekah, could she be Isaac's wife?
Rebekah drew water, gave drink to the camels, all of ten
Informed Abraham's servant she's the daughter of Bethuel.

Answer to prayer this could be Isaac's bride
To meet her family, he went with bride price
Rebekah's brother Laban ran to meet the man
Who came to take Rebekah for the son of Abraham.

The servant gave gifts to the family of Rebekah
Jewels of silver and gold to her brother and mother
Rebekah left with the servant to become Isaac's wife
So Isaac and Rebekah became partners for life.

LESSON

> ➤ Prayer is key when seeking a life time partner.
> ➤ Seek godly guidance when making important decisions.

PRAYER

Lord, in my search for a life's partner or any important thing needed in my life please lead and direct me in Jesus name.

FOCUS PSALM
PSALM 24:6

*This is the generation of them that seek him
that seek thy face, O Jacob. Selah.*

ADDITIONAL PRAYER POINTS AND DECLARATIONS BASED ON GENESIS 24

1. Lord, God of heaven and earth provide a good spouse for me/ my friend in Jesus name [24:3]
2. Lord, help me to keep the vow I made to you in Jesus name [24:9].
3. Lord, send your angel before me today to remove every obstacle to my progress today in Jesus name [24:7]
4. O Lord, I pray for your divine guidance in this matter [name it] in Jesus name [24:7]
5. Blessed be the Lord God of Abraham, who leads and guide me [24:27]
6. I will take care of the animals in my possession [24:11].
7. Lord, in Jesus name be with us as we journey today [24:12].

8. Lord, provide room in our house so we can occasionally accommodate visitors to lodge in Jesus name [24:23].
9. Blessed be the Lord God of Abraham, lead me to the place I must go [24:27].
10. Lord, open my eyes to see the persons you have placed in my life to bless me in Jesus name [24:64].

GENESIS 24 QUIZ
ANSWER TRUE OR FALSE

1. Abraham made his servant swear that he would not allow his son to marry a Canaanite.   True/False
2. Abraham's servant prayed for God to show kindness to Abraham as he went in search for Isaac a wife.   True/False
3. On his journey to search for Isaac a wife the servant took 10 camels with him.   True/False
4. Rebekah was the daughter of Bethuel.   True/False
5. Laban was Rebecca father.   True/False
6. Rebekah gave Abraham's servant camels water in drink.   True/False
7. Abraham's servant did not give Rebekah's mother jewels of silver and gold.   True/False
8. Laban ask Rebekah if she would go with Abraham's servant to meet Isaac.   True/False
9. Isaac was meditating in the field when he saw the camels returning with Rebekah.   True/False
10. Isaac took Rachel for his wife.   True/False

GENESIS 25:1-18
POEM, PRAYERS AND DECLARATIONS

POEM
Death Of Abraham

Abraham gave Isaac all his possession
Isaac the son of promise, Sarah's one son.

Abraham the father of nations had many children
Sarah, Hagar and Keturah were the mothers of them.
Hagar gave birth to Ishmael, Abraham's first
Sarah gave birth to Isaac, the promise of the Lord.

Six children Abraham had with Keturah
Jakshan, Zimran, Medan, Midian, Ishbak and Shuah
Abraham gave Isaac all his possession
Isaac, the son of promise, Sarah one son.

Unto the sons of Keturah, he gave some gifts
Then sent them away eastward, there they lived.
Isaac lived with his father until he died
A hundred and fifty years were the time of Abraham's life.

In the cave of Machpelah Isaac and Ishmael buried him
The same field Abraham's wife was buried in.

LESSON

➢ It is wise to leave an inheritance for your children.
➢ Make burial preparation for your family at the appropriate time.
➢ Take care of the elderly persons of your household and family.

PRAYER

Lord, bless me so that I can be a blessing to others.

FOCUS PSALM
PSALM 25; 12-13

12 What man is he that feareth the Lord? him shall he teach in the way that he shall choose.
13 His soul shall dwell at ease; and his seed shall inherit the earth.

ABRAHAM AND SARAH IN SOME OTHER BOOKS OF THE BIBLE

Abraham
James 2:21
Acts 3:25
Hebrews 11:8
Matthew 1:1
Galatians 3:8
Romans 4:1
Galatians 4:22

Sarah
1 Peter 3:6
Romans 9:9
Hebrews 11:11-12
Romans 4:19
Galatians 4:30

ADDITIONAL PRAYER POINTS AND DECLARATIONS BASED ON GENESIS 25

1. (For the single person). Heavenly Father, lead and direct me in choosing a good life time partner in Jesus name. Show me the person and tell me their name, in the name of Jesus Christ [25:1].
2. Lord, bring comfort to the widow/widowers among us in the name of Jesus Christ [25:1].
3. (For the married person). Heavenly Father thank you for my wife/husband, I pray that You touch her/him in a special way today, in Jesus name [25:1].
4. Lord, remember the boys (sons, nephews, brothers, cousins etc) in our family; protect, save and guide them in the name of Jesus Christ [25:4].
5. Lord, bless me and put me in a position to bless my family and friends in Jesus name [25:5].
6. Lord, fill my life and hands with gifts to present to others in Jesus name [25:5].
7. (For parents) I will be a parent of godly children in Jesus name [25:4].
8. I choose to be a blessing to those around me in the name of Jesus Christ. [25:5].

GENESIS 25:14-28
POEM, PRAYERS AND DECLARATIONS

POEM
A Husband Prays For His Wife

Isaac was forty years old when he took Rebekah for a wife
He prayed the Lord for her to get pregnant
and bring forth a child.
Rebekah got pregnant with twins, yes, with twins!
In her belly the children struggled with in.

"Why is this" she enquired of the Lord, the Heavenly Father.
The Lord said "two nations are within you,
one shall be stronger than the other".
It was now time, the twins to deliver
Out came Esau, the first born, red hair all over.

Out came the other son holding his brother heel.
Jacob they called him, second addition to the family.
Esau became a hunter but Jacob just a plain man
The father favoured Esau but mother the other son.

One day Esau came from the field faint and hungry
He came just in time, for Jacob pot of food was ready.
Feed me I pray with some of that food, Esau cried.
"Of course, if you sell me your birthright," Jacob replied.

Esau so hungry, agreed to this
Sold his birthright for a pot of food, can you imagine this?
A pot of food, that's all it meant to him
But Jacob, he knew the birthright benefit.

LESSON

> ➢ Desire good things.
> ➢ Husbands should pray for their wives.
> ➢ Do not take your spiritual inheritance for granted.
> ➢ Be kind to your siblings/love ones

PRAYER

Lord, may we cherish our spiritual heritage and
desire the good things you have in store for us

FOCUS PSALM
PSALM 25:14

The secret of the Lord is with them that fear
him; and he will shew them his covenant.

ADDITIONAL PRAYER POINTS AND DECLARATIONS BASED ON GENESIS 25

1. Lord, bless me and put me in a position to bless my family and friends in Jesus name [25:5].
2. I choose to be a blessing to someone today in Jesus name.
3. Lord, remember the couples in our church, bless their marriages and make them fruitful in Jesus name [25:21].
4. Lord, lead the husbands to pray for their wives as Isaac prayed for Rebekah in Jesus name [25:21].
5. As God answered Rebekah so He will answer me. God answers prayers [25:22].
6. I enquired of the Lord and He answered me [25:22].
7. Lord, in Jesus name deliver each parent from any ungodly attitude towards their children [25:26].

8. Lord, may our sons (boys in our family) grow to become strong godly young men with a good profession in Jesus name [25:27].
9. Lord, help us to look out for the best interest of our family in Jesus name [25:31].

GENESIS 25 QUIZ
ANSWER TRUE OR FALSE

1. Abraham's third wife name was Keturah.   True/False
2. Abraham died at 150 years old.   True/False
3. Isaac and Ishmael buried Abraham in the
   cave of Machpelah.   True/False
4. Isaac was 46 years old when he took Rachel
   for a wife.   True/False
5. Isaac prayed for his wife because she was barren. True/False
6. Rachel had twin boys, Esau and Cain.   True/False
7. Esau was born before Jacob.   True/False
8. Jacob was born holding his brothers heel.   True/False
9. During Rebekah's pregnancy her twins
   struggled together in her womb.   True/False
10. The Lord said that Rebekah's sons represented
    two nations and two manner of people.   True/False

ISAAC AND REBEKAH IN SOME OTHER BOOKS OF THE BIBLE
Matthew 1:2
Hebrew 11:20
James 2:21
Hebrews 11:17
Galatians 4:28-31

SECTION 3

TOPICAL PRAYERS BASED ON
THE BOOK OF GENESIS

PRAYER FOR FAMILY

1. Lord, remember us as a couple, may we keep your commandments and not be deceived by the devil as Adam and Eve were in Jesus name.
2. Lord, let there be peace in our family. Do not allow any family member to commit murder or any crime against the other as in the case of Cain and Abel.
3. Lord, keep my household in righteousness as you kept Noah's household in Jesus name.
4. Lord any family you are directing to change location or to migrate, may they heed to your Word and move by faith as Abram and Sarai did.
5. Lord, protect our family from sibling rivalry and parental favouritism in the name of Jesus Christ. Do not allow what took place in Jacob's family to occur in ours, in the name of Jesus.
6. Lord, may love reign in my family as each member look out for the best interest of the other; may we treat each other with love and not as Joseph's brothers treated him in an unkind manner.
7. Lord, protect my family from every kind of criminal behavior and do not allow us be victims of crime as portrayed in the case of Tamar, Jacobs's daughter in Jesus name.
8. Lord, free my family from deception and lies that was evident in Jacob and Abraham's household. Let truth reign in this family in Jesus name.
9. Lord, let your blessings be upon my family in finances, property and posterity [children] as You did for Abraham in Jesus name.
10. I break and lose myself and my family from every curse in the name of Jesus Christ.

PRAYER OF A WIFE

1. Lord, in Jesus name forgive me if I have led or encouraged my husband to sin as Eve did Adam.
2. Lord, in Jesus name help my husband to develop a good relationship with You and to know Your voice as Abraham did.
3. Lord Jesus, help my husband to be a good provider for the family, to lead the family in spiritual matters and to dispel any strife that may arise between us as a couple and family as You helped Abraham in such circumstances.
4. Lord let me be a fruitful wife like Sarai, Rebekah and Rachel, remember me as you remembered them and open my womb in Jesus name.
5. Lord deal strongly with every situation that poses a threat to my relationship with my husband as you dealt with Abraham and Sarai situations with Hagar and Abimelech in Jesus name.
6. Lord in Jesus name help me to be submissive to my husband as a good wife should like Sarah.

PRAYER TO SEIZE OPPORTUNITIES

1. Lord, help me to seize opportunities presented to me as did our forefathers in Genesis in Jesus name.
2. Lord, may I seize the opportunity to build an altar of prayer, a place and time of worship as Noah, Abraham, and Jacob in Jesus name.
3. Lord, may I seize the opportunity to show you off, to show your mighty power as Joseph seize the opportunity to show that you are an interpreter of dreams.
4. Lord, like Joseph may I seize the opportunity to excel.
5. Lord, like Abraham interceded for Sodom, may I seize the opportunity to intercede for others in Jesus name.

6. Lord, may I seize the opportunity to make amends with persons who have hurt me as Esau seize the opportunity to do so with Jacob in Jesus name.

7. Lord, may I seize the opportunity to be the spouse of a godly partner with your guidance and direction as Rebekah did in Jesus name.

8. Lord, may I seize the opportunities of open doors leading to freedom as Noah went out of the ark on dry land in Jesus name.

9. Lord, may I seize the opportunity of forgiveness and repentance as Jacob did with his brother Esau in Jesus name.

10. Lord, may I seize the opportunities to give and be a blessing as Abraham did in the case of Melchizedek in Jesus name.

11. I seize the good opportunities the Lord presents before me in the name of Jesus Christ, opportunities for greater blessings, promotion, freedom and deliverance in the name of Jesus Christ.

PRAYER FOR PROVISIONS

1. Lord, provide for me food as you did for Adam and Eve in abundance in the name of Jesus Christ.

2. Lord, provide for me good clothing as you did for Adam and Eve.

3. Lord, provide shelter as you did for those in Noah's ark in Jesus name.

4. Lord, provide us with ownership of land and property as you did for Abraham in Jesus name.

5. Lord, provide guidance and direction as you did for Abraham and his family in Canaan in Jesus name.

6. Lord, provide water to drink for person who need it, as you did for Ishmael and Hagar in the desert in Jesus name.

PRAYER FOR A VISITATION FROM GOD

1. God of wonder, might love and power I desire a visitation from your today.
2. Visit me Lord, even in my times of weakness and clothe me in righteousness as you did Adam in Jesus name.
3. Visit me Lord as you did Abraham and show me what to do and where to go in Jesus name.
4. Lord, visit me and let your presence be known as you did Abram and Sarai, and cause me to rejoice in Jesus name.
5. Visit me Lord and remind me of your promises and power in the name of Jesus Christ.
6. Let your presence be known and evident with me O mighty God, I pray for a divine visitation in the name of Jesus Christ.

PRAYER FOR HELP

1. Lord, my present help in times of trouble help me today in the name of Jesus Christ.
2. Lord show up in my life as my helper and my God.
3. Help me Lord, as you helped Adam and Eve in their times of sinfulness, give me new garments, take away the old sinful clothes and clothes me in your righteousness in the name of Jesus.
4. Help me Lord, in situations of strife as you helped Abram when he experience strife with his herd men and Lot, to make the right choices for peace and safety me Lord.
5. Help me to escape places of wickedness and corruption as you helped Lot out of such situations.
6. Help me Lord as you helped Noah to build a place of safety for me and my family to be secure in you in the name of Jesus.
7. Help me Lord in the name of Jesus as you helped Isaac to get a life partner, I need your help O Lord.

8. Help me Lord to survive times of hardship and famine as you helped Jacob in the name of Jesus.

9. Lord God help me to get out of every pit-like and prison-like situation as you helped Joseph.

10. I receive help from the Lord in the name of Jesus Christ.

PRAYER FOR HOPE

1. My hope is in you Lord God of Abraham and Isaac.

2. Restore my hope in you God and take away any sense of hopelessness in the name of Jesus Christ.

3. Build up my hope in you Lord as you did for Abraham in times of hopelessness when he thought he would remain childless, build up my hope and expectation of you Almighty God in the name of Jesus.

4. Lord God, build up my hope and confidence in You, for you are a God of miracles and wonders as seen in the days of creation and Abraham in the name of Jesus Christ.

5. By speaking your Word in the beginning, the heavens and earth came into being; speak a word in my life Lord God, restore my confidence and hope in you, in the name of Jesus Christ.

6. Even in this world of wickedness build up my hope Lord God of miracles and wonders in the name of Jesus Christ.

7. By your Word Lord, restore my hope; by your promises restore my faith; by your power restore my confidence in you in the name of Jesus Christ.

PRAYER FOR DELIVERANCE

1. Deliver me Lord from wickedness as You delivered Noah the name of Jesus Christ.

2. Deliver me Lord from barrenness and unfruitfulness as you did Sarah, deliver me from a barren and unfruitful life in the name of Jesus Christ. May I be a fruitful Christian in the name of Jesus.

3. Deliver me Lord from famine and drought as you delivered Abraham in the name of Jesus Christ.

4. In the name of Jesus Christ, Heavenly Father delivered me from bondage as you did Lot, when he was captured by King Chedoloamer.

5. Deliver me Lord, from strife and contention as you delivered Abram in the name of Jesus Christ.

6. Deliver me Lord, from sickness and curses as you did Abimelech in the name of Jesus Christ.

7. Deliver me Lord from deception and trickery the in name of Jesus Christ.

8. Deliver me O Lord from hopelessness as you delivered Abram in from unfruitfulness in the name of Jesus Christ.

9. I receive my deliverance now in the name of Jesus Christ.

10. I am delivered from drought, famine, unfruitfulness, strife, sickness, deception, hopelessness and shame etc. in the name of Jesus Christ.

REFERENCE

The Bible, Authorize King James Version

STEPS TO SALVATION

If you are not born again, meaning you have not accepted Jesus Christ as your personal Savior and Lord and you would like to do so, please say this prayer with sincerity of heart.

Heavenly Father, I admit I am a sinner and I want to be saved, forgive me of all sins. I believe Jesus Christ the son of God died on the cross for my sins and rose from the dead. I accept Him as my Savior and Lord. Save me Father in Jesus name. I now receive the gift of eternal life.

ENCOURAGEMENT IN YOUR WALK WITH GOD

- Reading your Bible and pray every day.
- Go to church regularly and participate in church activities.
- Use this book to help you pray and explore the book of Genesis.

ACKNOWLEDGEMENT

All praise and glory to the Almighty God for granting me the opportunity as an instrument of His to pen this book. Thanks to those persons who helped to make this book a reality. Special thanks to my husband Donald, my family and friends for your love and unwavering support. Thanks to Gillian Whyte for your invaluable assistance, and recommendations from the initial stages of this book.

ABOUT THE AUTHOR

Melecia Davis-Gibbs (DTh.) is a Pastor, Lecturer and Counselor who has been in full time ministry for over fifteen years. She has served the body of Christ in various capacities such as, Worship Leader, Intercessor, Evangelism and Missions Coordinator. As a Bible College Lecturer some of the courses she has taught are Pentateuch, Poetics Books, Pauline Epistles, General Epistle, Hermeneutics and Typology.

Rev. Davis-Gibbs is a seminar and conference speaker known for her simple but profound presentations on topics such as Spiritual Fruits, Spiritual Gifts, Prayer, Worship Leading and Evangelism. She has a passion for teaching the Word of God and seeing persons apply it to their lives.